Beyond Mormonism

An Elder's Story

Dedicated to Margaretta,
Erin and Jaime

Beyond Mormonism

An Elder's Story

James R. Spencer

Published by
chosen books

FLEMING H. REVELL COMPANY
TARRYTOWN, NEW YORK

Some of the names in this book have been changed to protect the privacy of the people involved.

Unless otherwise indicated, the Bible translation quoted is the Rivised Standard Version, copyright © 1946 and 1952 by Division of Christian Education of the National Council of the churches of Christ in the United States of America.

Library of Congress Cataloging in Publication Data

Spencer, James R.
    Beyond Mormonism.

    Bibliography: p.

    1. Spencer, James R.   2. Mormons—United States—Biograpny.   3. Converts—United States—Biography.   4. Mormon Church—Controversial literature.   5. Church of Jesus Christ of Latter-Day Saints—Controversial literature.   I. Title.
BX8695.S76A34 1984   289.3'3   [B]   84-9633
ISBN 0-8007-9076-6

A Chosen Book

Copyright © 1984 James R. Spencer

Chosen Books are Published by
Fleming H. Revell Company
Old Tappan, New Jersey
Printed in the United States of America

Contents

Acknowledgments

Thanks to Mary Lebrecht and Linda Cox for the hours of typing. For important thoughtful suggestions: Dick and Jan Landis; my editor, Jane Campbell; and my wife, Margaretta. For bearing with me: the congregation at Shiloh. And for covering for me: the leadership team at Shiloh. Without these gracious people, this book would not have been completed.

1

LOOKING FOR A LIFELINE

Sixteen serious-looking high priests eyed me intently from the perimeter of a horseshoe formed by three long tables set in a sparsely furnished room. My wife fidgeted in the chair on my left. On my right, Bishop Addison, charged with protecting my rights, absently drummed his fingers on the wooden chair arm.

Six high priests of the Church of Jesus Christ of Latter-day Saints sat along each leg of the horseshoe. The stake president, assisted by his two counselors and clerk, conducted the meeting. The priests appeared to me to be as hard and austere as the oak tables and chairs, and reflected the uncompromising structure of the organization that now brought me to trial. The atmosphere produced in me a bone-aching weariness.

The stake president adjusted his glasses and studied a sheaf of papers. He looked up at me, cleared his throat and began to read.

"This duly constituted court of the Yellowstone Stake of the Church of Jesus Christ of Latter-day Saints," he began, "is convened to investigate charges that Elder James R. Spencer is guilty of conduct in violation of the law and order of the Church."

I was on trial for apostasy, charged with abandoning the faith. Apostasy is the most serious failing for a Mormon, and doubly grave when the apostate is, as I was, an elder—a bearer of the Holy Melchizedek Priesthood. My penalty for apostasy would be excommunication—to be cut off from the Church. In a community 75 percent Mormon, excommunication means social as well as spiritual ostracism. Excommunicated Mormons become modern-day untouchables. They lose their friends, often their jobs, sometimes even their families. I looked at my wife, Margaretta. What was she thinking?

The president recounted that I had joined the Mormon Church in 1964. As an active Mormon for ten years, I had served in many responsible positions in the Church. I had been a counselor to the Sunday school superintendent, stake missionary and youth worker. And I served with zeal. For five years I taught gospel doctrine classes for the Church, conducting the largest and most popular classes in the community. Men much older than myself—former bishops and even a stake president—attended my classes. My excommunication would be a community scandal.

Excommunication is the final judgment of the Mormon Church. An excommunicant, in addition to losing all other rights in the Church, is forbidden even to speak in church. He is denied Communion. He cannot pay tithes. If he holds the Melchizedek Priesthood, and if he will not repent, he will, according to Church doctrine, be cast into outer darkness with Satan and his angels where there is "only weeping, wailing and gnashing of teeth."

At the request of the stake president, Margaretta was witnessing my excommunication. I could only guess what

was going through her mind. But I knew this public humiliation was painful and embarrassing for her. Everything that
had occurred in recent months had torn at the fabric of our
relationship and strained our marriage.

What had happened to me was unheard of. We were
stalwarts in the faith, "True Believers." We were temple
Mormons, privileged to the innermost secrets of the
Church. And there was no question as to my character,
faithfulness or religious zeal. My enthusiasm for God,
study of the Bible, duty to my family—all these had actually
intensified over the last two years, so that it struck me as
ironic that I should be on trial for abandoning the faith.

But because of my position in the Church, I had seen
some of the inner workings of Mormondom that troubled
me deeply. These had triggered some philosophical and
doctrinal questions that led me, after exhaustive research,
to make the most difficult decision of my life.

Now, as President Jones continued to read, and as the
proceedings approached the point at which I would need to
make a verbal response to the charges, I reflected on what
had brought me to this time and place. Had it only been ten
years since I had joined the Mormon Church? My expecta-
tions had been so high. The Church had offered so much
promise, so much hope for the emptiness I had known.

No one seeing me deplane from an Alaskan jet at the Los
Angeles International Airport would have guessed I was a
candidate for religion. I did not look like part of any estab-
lishment, civil or religious. I stepped into the smog and
noise of Los Angeles with a six-month growth of beard,
wearing faded blue jeans, a sweater and sports jacket. A
half-pint of scotch stuck out of my jacket pocket. Pinned to
my lapel was a small sign clipped from *Mad Magazine* that
read, "I'm not a beatnik—just a bum."

In the fall of 1964 hippies were still beatniks; the flower children had not yet invaded Haight-Ashbury; John Kennedy was gone (but not Robert or Martin Luther King); the riots in Watts were a couple months away; and the Vietnam War was still little known.

Recently discharged from the Navy, I was living life to the fullest, grabbing for all the gusto I could get. That meant women, gambling and booze, in that order. I traveled where I wanted, when I wanted.

Outside, in front of the terminal, I lit a cigarette and waited for my luggage. After three months in the clean air of Alaska, the acrid afternoon air of Los Angeles made the cigarette taste strange. I was back in L.A., all right; the automobile traffic and jet noise were deafening. From a pay phone I made a date for late that night with a girl I had met two weeks before I left for Alaska. Then I grabbed a cab and headed for Gardena.

The Horseshoe Club was alive with people when I got there mid-evening. I walked over to the chalkboard and under the "$2.00-$4.00" category wrote *X. X. Jones*, the pseudonym I always used in the card houses. Then I ordered a scotch at the bar while I waited for my name to be called for a place at a table.

Overlooking the playing floor, I watched the gamblers playing "California Draw" and "Lowball." The smoke was thick and the felt gaming tables looked like little green islands with people clinging to the edges. Some of the players looked as though they had been there since morning.

I had begun to play poker seriously in the Navy and had spent thousands of hours around poker tables. Before my enlistment was over, I was winning regularly. In fact, during the last year of my enlistment I actually made more money gambling than I did from my pay as an electronics technician.

After leaving the Navy I returned to my hometown in Wyoming and worked for a summer in the oilfields. But soon I returned to L.A., got a job in the electronics industry and spent nearly every night in the card houses. For several months I had gambled professionally, spending my full time in the card houses of Gardena and occasionally driving to Cabazon, a small town near Palm Springs where gambling was also legal.

When a spot opened up for me to join in the action I killed my scotch, winked at the barmaid and left her a five-dollar tip. *Seed money,* I thought to myself.

The snap of the cards from the fingers of the passive-faced dealer punctuated the serious silence of the game. With seven players, the average pot on the "2-4" tables was thirty to sixty dollars.

I fingered the heavy plastic chips embossed with the gold Horseshoe Club logo. I loved the click of them. I liked the way they handled, heavy in the hand, and how they landed firm on the foam-padded green felt. And I never lost my fascination for the way the cards fanned on the surface of the table under the deft fingernail of the winner as he unveiled his hand and raked in the pot with one smooth movement.

Nobody spoke at the tables except for an occasional expletive or phrase of complaint—"Two ladies," "Aces over," "Couldn't catch a spade. . . ."

Angela arrived at 10:00, right on time. I talked her into having a drink alone while I played a couple more hands. At midnight, after three warnings from Angela, I took three neat stacks of chips to the cashier. One hundred eighty dollars. After an initial buy-in of fifty dollars, I had made $130 in three-and-a-half hours.

At 4:30 a.m., I stood on the balcony of Angela's sixth-floor apartment overlooking the darkened city of Glendale. The pre-dawn air was smogless and almost fresh. In the distance I heard the night sirens. From somewhere below, angry voices worked their way into the night sounds of the city. A glow in the sky marked downtown Los Angeles five miles to the south.

I was home. At least, I wanted to think so. But I remembered that I had left L.A. in the spring looking for something I hoped to find in Alaska. At first I had been overwhelmed by the quiet beauty of the green-black shores that unfolded as the S.S. Puffin plied the dark waters of the Gulf of Alaska. But I was looking for something beyond beauty and solitude, something more than a few months away from the city. I was looking for something deep inside myself—a hungry longing for something I couldn't even name.

Standing now in the pre-dawn light on Angela's balcony, peering over the dark city, I remembered the pre-dawns I had spent leaning on the lifeline of the Puffin watching the phosphorus swirls in the dark water. Watching the black line of the horizon, smoking in silence, thinking. I was looking for something, but *what was it?*

I recalled nights spent in Anchorage bars—scenes that blended with scenes from bars in L.A. and Acapulco and Manila and Hong Kong and San Pedro and Norfolk. I had traveled over half the world, from Central America to the Orient, from Maine to California, from Mexico to Alaska. I had looked into life, but I had a nagging suspicion that I had not really glimpsed it. Though I pursued life with youthful gusto, I had to admit I did not really feel alive.

Much of my life was an act—keeping up a macho front for my friends. Outwardly I tried to appear tough and sharp and self-assured, but inside I felt disappointed and lonely. I wandered and drank and read and played my guitar. And I wrote of my feelings in poetry I never showed anyone:

> Loneliness comes in the strangest of places,
> In a sea of laughing, unfriendly faces;
> Or with wind and rain at midnight.

During the past summer on the Gulf of Alaska I had grown restless, realizing that something was missing in my life. I was experiencing a growing weariness. Some nights, making my way in the dark along the lifelines as I headed for my bunk, I would listen to the rhythmic spray of cold water on the wooden hull of the Puffin. Staring out into the blackness I could almost feel a cold call, like some diabolical whisper from an alien world, drawing me.

That same summer I had read an editorial in *Look* magazine written by Erich Fromme. He said Americans were empty people trying to satisfy basic needs with chemicals and experiences. Fromme spoke of people who pumped alcohol and tobacco and drugs into their bodies and grabbed at illicit sex in a futile attempt to find satisfaction. At least for me, Fromme was right. I found myself, along with millions of other Americans, saying in the words of the rock song, "I can't get no satisfaction." For me life was becoming a meaningless trip. Everything seemed flat and pale.

As I continued to stare into the night from my perch above Glendale, I reached into the pocket of my jeans and extracted a wrinkled letter. It was from my old friend Lee. We had gone to high school together. He now lived in Palos Verdes, a peninsula sticking out into the Pacific near Los Angeles.

It was a strange letter. One line in it haunted me. "Jim," it read, "I have found the truth!" Lee said he had had a religious experience that changed his life. He wanted to talk to me about it.

Lee and I had spent many long nights trying to make sense out of our existence. We had talked of God, but reached no concrete conclusions as to how we really fit into the universe.

I had studied religion and occult phenomena all my life. I read every religious book I could get my hands on. I studied Catholicism and read Thomas à Kempis' *Imitation of Christ*. With a Buddhist girlfriend in Yokosuka, I studied Nichiren-sho-shu Buddhism (Soka-gakkai), chanting the "namu Myoho renge-kyo." I read all of D. T. Suzuki's works on Zen Buddhism. I was into hypnotism and ESP. I had been a serious student of hypnosis since the age of twelve. I had developed occult expertise to the point of being able to recognize colors with my fingertips.

But learning did not fill my emptiness. Spiritual knowledge did not satisfy my inner longings. Something was missing. I was growing discouraged with the prospect of ever finding meaning for my life. I was beginning to believe that the French existentialist Jean-Paul Sartre was right—that man was alone. That he had no past and no future. That religion was simply an attempt to escape the responsibility of living with the truth—which, when all was said and done, was that man is absolutely and finally alone.

Lee had always been important to me. He was the brightest, toughest guy I knew. If I would listen to anything anyone had to say, it would be Lee.

On the other hand, I was skeptical. What Lee was telling me seemed incredible—all the more so since I was familiar with the religious group Lee had joined. In fact, when I first got his letter I thought he had gone off the deep end, become a religious fanatic. My old buddy, my highly respected intellectual friend, had joined the Mormon Church!

Lee and I had grown up in Wyoming—Mormon country. Although I had never looked closely at Mormonism, I was sure that if any religion held the answer to my problems, Mormonism was not it. But his letter sounded so different—so sure, so sincere. Lee told me he had found "the truth." His search had come to an end. And he invited me to come listen to him.

So now, standing on the balcony overlooking Glendale, I had mixed emotions about visiting Lee the next day. Yet I had known from the moment I got the letter that I would listen to what Lee had to say. I would even give him a fair hearing. I was desperate. Something had to happen in my life, sooner than later.

Stuffing the letter back into my jeans, I crushed my cigarette on the metal railing and returned to bed.

2

A GLIMMER OF HOPE

Riding down the Harbor Freeway toward Palos Verdes, I felt the warm afternoon sun on my hand draped over Angela's shoulder. The distinctive purr of the MG motor rumbled in through the open windows. Angela brushed her blowing hair away from her eyes. The wind and motor noise precluded conversation. It was an hour's drive to Pacific Coast Highway and up the back of the hill to Lee's trailer on a large undeveloped lot overlooking the ocean.

According to our plan, the three of us would have dinner in Palos Verdes, after which Angela would drive back home to Glendale. Lee would take me to my mother's home in Santa Ana the following day to pick up my car.

I looked forward to seeing him, and couldn't help remembering our childhood in the barren little high-desert community of Basin in north-central Wyoming. When the dry August winds blew off the badlands of the Torchlight oilfields, Lee and Fred Johnson and I would spend our days on the muddy Big Horn River, fishing, rafting or swimming, and exploring the caves of nearby Deadhorse Gulch.

My family had pioneered that part of the state. My grandfather had opened the first general store in Basin. My grandmother had been instrumental in building St. Andrew's Episcopal Church in Basin, where I was baptized when I was five. In time I had been confirmed and served as an acolyte, helping the minister serve Communion. I remember sitting on the polished oak pews of St. Andrew's, listening in rapt attention to the minister speak of eternity. The hymns and prayers touched me.

My parents' stormy marriage ended in divorce the year I turned twelve. I had been an excellent student, but following the divorce my grades fell, my attitude became sullen and I dropped out of school my junior year of high school to join the Navy.

In the first year after my discharge, while I worked for an electronics company near San Bernardino, Lee worked in the construction business and was about to form his own company. We spent lots of time together, drinking some, trying out various techniques on girls, and I, of course, playing poker.

But we recognized, in many late-night talks that turned to God, that our hedonism was futile. One night Lee told me he had heard a rumor that our friend Fred Johnson had made a commitment to Jesus Christ in a Billy Graham Crusade in Kansas City. We didn't know what to make of that.

As Angela and I pulled into Lee's driveway high atop Palos Verdes peninsula, we were met by two big Labradors showing teeth. Getting out of the sports car, I offered them the back of my hand. They recognized me immediately and became friendly. Lee's truck was nowhere in sight.

We walked up to the mobile home set on blocks under a large shade tree. Under the trailer I could see boxes of old bottles, silverware and other antiques—all part of Lee's collection. The door, as always, was open. Inside, in the refrigerator, I found a six-pack of beer. At least my Mormon friend hadn't completely lost his mind!

Soon we heard Lee's pickup bouncing up the lane. The dogs began barking excitedly. From the front door I saw them circling the truck, wagging their tails, jumping up and barking as Lee stepped out of the truck. He grinned at us and waved, threw his hard hat into the back of the pickup, stopped to acknowledge each dog, then strode toward the trailer. He was big—six feet, about 220 pounds, and barrel-chested. Though Lee was only 22, his hair was already thinning.

Inside the trailer he threw his lunch bucket on the table and gave me a bear hug. "Long time no see, hombre!" Then, turning to Angela: "And what have we here! Spencer, where *did* you find this beautiful young lady?"

"Get a grip on yourself, man!" I held up the can in my hand. "Say, I helped myself to a beer."

"Good," Lee responded. "I don't drink anymore, but I like to keep something around for friends."

"Don't give me that. You may have gone off the deep end of the religious pier, but you haven't given up scotch and water."

Lee smiled. "Yes, I have."

"Give me a break! Lee, I'm not sure I want to talk to you anymore."

"Drink up while I shower, then let's grab some supper. Those of us who work for a living are hungry!" To Angela he added, "I ought to warn you about Spencer. He's fickle and untrustworthy. He'll bring you to a bad end."

"Go take a shower, Lee."

"Yeah," said Angela. "Cool down!"

"Oh, I *like* her, Jimmie!"

We had supper at the foot of Palos Verdes, on Pacific Coast Highway. Then I kissed Angela goodbye and promised to call her in a couple days.

When Lee and I returned to the trailer, we walked to a brow overlooking the ocean. The moon was nearly full and almost overhead. The waters of the Pacific crashed far below. The gray line of the horizon was visible against the black of the night sky. I lit up a Viceroy. Lee shook off my offer of a cigarette. We were both quiet.

"O.K., man. Tell me about it."

Lee looked out toward the distant horizon. Something did seem different about him. It wasn't just the fact that I had not seen him take a drink. Or the fact that he didn't smoke. Or even that I had not heard him swear all evening. But I had known Lee since he moved to Basin in the sixth grade. We had shared our first drink together. We had fixed up an old '37 Chevrolet and driven it forty miles a weekend to court a pair of sisters in Lovell. Mormon girls, I seemed to remember. Lee and I were like brothers. And now there was definitely something different about him—more peaceful, maybe.

"I don't know, Jim. It's really strange. I don't know if you'll understand, but I have to try."

"I *want* you to try."

Lee chuckled. "Remember the fifth of tequila under the Russian olive tree in Basin?"

"Of course I do!"

Silence. "Last spring, Jim, I took a trip home to Wyoming. I had a couple weeks off. Wanted to be home for Dad's birthday." Lee looked straight ahead and his voice grew soft. "I stopped in St. George, Utah, for a sandwich. I got into this conversation with the waitress and asked her out for a drink when she got off work. She told me she didn't drink, but would be glad to have a Coke with me when she got off.

"Jimmie, we talked until two in the morning. I know you're going to think this is crazy, but when she told me the story—the *real* story of the Mormons—I knew she was telling me the truth."

"What do you mean, you knew?"

"It's hard to explain. But as she talked to me I had this feeling. She was telling me about the early history of the Church. And as she spoke, all I knew was that she was saying something I needed to hear. Anyway, that was the start of my investigation. I promised her that when I got back to California I'd get in touch with the Mormon missionaries and have them teach me about the Mormon Church. You know, hear them out. Well, I went through six of what the Church calls 'discussions' with the missionaries."

"What were these discussions about?"

"I want to go into that with you. But let me say right off the bat that I'm not an expert in these things. Matter of fact, I've only been a member of the Church for about six weeks. I've got a lot to learn. But at first, you know, I was very skeptical." He glanced at me. "Like you are right now."

"You noticed."

Lee laughed. "Hey, I don't blame you! Just don't close your mind, O.K.?"

We talked into the wee hours of the morning. Lee told me of his discussions with the missionaries. How he had searched his heart. And how one night, when things were weighing heavily on him, he had climbed the fence of a football stadium and, sitting alone in the bleachers, made the decision to join the Mormon Church. He knew he had made the right decision. And I could tell Lee was fully convinced.

As he finished what he called his "testimony," Lee turned to me. The moonlight revealed a tear edging slowly down his cheek.

"I've found the truth, Jim. I tell you I *know,* by the power of the Holy Ghost, that Jesus is the Christ; that Joseph Smith, the founder of the Church, was a prophet of God; and that the Mormon Church is God's only True Church today."

I didn't like what Lee said. I liked less the way he said it. It made me uncomfortable.

But Lee was unequivocal and passionate. "Jim," he said, "this is what we've been searching for."

"Lee, I don't know where you're coming from. I can see that something important has happened to you, but frankly, I can't imagine you have found the truth in the Mormon Church."

"I know what you mean, Jim. I had the same doubts. Listen, I'm not able to explain myself very well. I want you to talk to the missionaries."

"I'm always open to new ideas, Lee. You know that. But don't get your hopes up. This Mormonism stuff sounds pretty spooky to me." I slapped him on the shoulder. "Hey, you have to work tomorrow. I'm going to think about what you've said. And I *will* talk to these missionaries. Listen, I want to watch the water for a while, so why don't you hit the hay? Let me sleep in the morning. I'll catch a cab to the Horseshoe Club when I wake up and you can meet me there after work. Then I can catch a ride to Mom's in Santa Ana."

Lee rose and laid a hand on my shoulder. "Sure thing, man. I'll pick you up around seven." He grinned. "Don't spend that entire Alaskan bankroll in one place."

As Lee's footsteps faded into the night behind me, I looked at the beautiful buttermilk clouds silhouetting the moon. Fifteen miles out in the San Pedro Channel, a freighter cleared Santa Catalina and made her way into Long Beach Harbor.

I didn't know what to make of Lee's experience. He said he had found the truth. Inwardly I hoped there *was* such a thing as truth. Lee had asked me not to close my mind. That was reasonable enough. At least I believed there was a God. Maybe it was just a holdover from my childhood in St. Andrews, but in the last few years, even as I became less certain who God was, I became more certain *that* He was.

I had a haunting sense that God was trying somehow to point me toward truth. In recent years I had had a number of intense experiences in which I had, as Lee put it, felt close to Him.

One was a near-death experience in the Gulf of Alaska when an unexpected gale had hit. Our ship, while rolling dangerously, had somehow, miraculously, not capsized. Though I had sailed thousands of miles in heavy weather and seen lots of whitewater on the bridge, I had never been in peril at sea; and the wonder of that reprieve remained fresh in my mind thirty days later.

A second brush with death had occurred just after my discharge from the Navy. While I was driving home blind drunk one night, I rolled my Chevrolet at ninety miles per hour. I was thrown through the windshield, and as the car slid sideways through the grass, I hung over the front fender with my feet tangled in the steering wheel. When the car began to roll one more time, I knew I would be crushed beneath it. But at the last second, it slammed back down on all four wheels and catapulted me high into the air. I landed on my head and shoulders, breaking only my collarbone.

As I lay there in the grass, my head bleeding, my shoes torn from my feet and my lungs feeling as though they had been punctured, a surprising feeling of peace flooded over me. I *knew* God had spared me.

A third, seemingly inconsequential experience had also had a profound impact on me spiritually. In Hong Kong three years earlier, the captain of our frigate had hired some impoverished Chinese men to paint the ship, paying them for their labor by allowing them to collect our garbage to feed their families. I can't explain the impact it made on me as a smiling worker scraped the contents of my dinner tray into different garbage cans—one can for meat, another for peas, another for bread.

Why, I cried out to God, was I in a position to give my slop to other men? I felt the humiliation of these Chinese fathers—men whose manhood seemed crushed as they silently collected garbage from rich American boys who seemed to have no greater concern than to hasten into Hong Kong to drink Tiger Ale in the brothels.

Now, in the still of the night high above the Pacific, I got up and walked back toward Lee's trailer. Reducing things to the barest minimum, I knew one thing and suspected another. First, I knew there was a God. Second, I thought He had spared my life for some reason. Twice in two years I had smelled the cold breath of death and I didn't like it.

Was God trying to show me something? And could that something be Mormonism?

3

THE HAND OF FELLOWSHIP

The two young men smiled pleasantly at me through the screen door. "Hi! Mr. Spencer? We're from the Church of Jesus Christ of Latter-day Saints."

My first thought was, *These aren't missionaries, they're kids!* Nevertheless, for Lee's sake, I ushered them into the living room. They introduced themselves as Elder Morgan from Alabama and Elder Jackson from Utah. Their dark suits, white shirts and "sidewall" haircuts did not impress me. Plus, I thought, they smiled too much. *Snake oil salesmen,* I said to myself.

Seating them in kitchen chairs, I sat down on the couch. I put my feet up on the coffee table and lit up a cigarette, hoping that would unnerve them. If it did, they didn't show it, but just continued to smile and make small talk.

It was my mother's apartment. Lee had dropped me off there a week earlier, the day after our conversation overlooking the ocean at Palos Verdes. The company I worked for in Alaska had offered me a job in Saudi Arabia, but I wanted to settle down for a while—maybe take some night classes at Santa Ana Junior College, since I had completed my high school requirements by correspondence—and find my own apartment.

"Well, men," I said, "my friend Lee probably has talked to you. I'm impressed with what I see in him, but I want you to know that I am not super-interested in Mormonism. However, I *did* tell Lee I would listen and remain objective. Lee said you have some 'discussions'?"

Elder Jackson seemed to be in charge. He was tall, blonde and self-assured. Opening a long plastic envelope that looked like a carrying case for a pool cue, he extracted a folding tripod and a display board covered with flannel. "I hope you won't mind if we use some pictures to illustrate our discussion?"

"As long as they're clean pictures!" I joked.

Elder Jackson grinned at me, but I thought I detected a tint of red in Elder Morgan's face.

Elder Jackson placed a strip reading *The Church of Jesus Christ* on the top of his flannel board. "Well, Mr. Spencer, there certainly are a lot of churches in the world today. Which church are you most familiar with?"

"I was raised Episcopalian, but I've also studied Catholicism."

"Why do you suppose there are so many churches?"

"I guess because there are so many different ideas about God."

"That's a really good answer. Take a simple thing like baptism. Some people believe it is necessary and some don't. Some believe it has to be done by immersion and others by sprinkling."

He placed a picture of Jesus on the flannel board. "Back when there were living prophets on the earth, how do you think the Lord gave men the answers to questions like this?"

It was a leading question, presupposing some things I wasn't ready to stipulate. But I didn't want to appear too hardheaded, so I replied, "I suppose He spoke to the people through the prophets."

"Exactly!"

I had to credit Elder Jackson with enthusiasm. You would have thought I had answered the $64,000 question, he acted so pleased.

"I'm sure you have wondered what it was like to live in ancient times. Tell me, suppose you *had* lived back then and had a question about religion. Why would you have gone to a prophet for an answer?"

"Well, if there were a prophet, I suppose I would have asked him because he'd be able to tell me what God thought about the question."

Elder Jackson beamed. "Why were the statements of the prophets so valuable?"

"Because a true prophet would have spoken for God."

"Do you think it was valuable to the people to have living prophets?"

What could I say? "Of course," I replied.

Drawing up his chair an inch, Elder Jackson looked into my eyes and asked, "Would a living prophet be valuable to the churches today? Would a living prophet be able to speak to us about the question of baptism, for instance?"

I felt uncomfortable, but for the life of me I couldn't seem to do anything but follow his lead. He was so confident, so polite. Besides, the things he said were not really *wrong*. I knew he was leading me, yet I didn't think he was out of line.

"Of course," I admitted, "a living prophet would be able to clear up questions about baptism."

Elder Jackson paused, got my full attention with his eyes and then began to speak. I was astounded at how much he reminded me of the way Lee looked and sounded when he had given his testimony a week earlier. The look in this man's eye, the manner of speech seemed canned. Though I was sure he was sincere, still it disturbed me.

"Mr. Spencer, the reason Elder Morgan and I are here today is to tell you about a prophet who was called by the Lord for our own time. His name was Joseph Smith.

"In 1820," he continued, "Joseph Smith was a young man living in the state of New York. He wanted to join a church, but as he visited those in his neighborhood he found confusion—similar to the things we've been talking about today.

"So he decided to pray and ask God which church was right. He went to a grove of trees near his father's farm and knelt in prayer. As he was praying he saw a pillar of light exactly over his head, above the brightness of the sun, which descended gradually until it fell upon him.

"When the light rested on him he saw, standing above him in the air, two personages in the form of men whose brightness and glory defied all description. One of them called Joseph Smith by name and said, 'This is My beloved Son.'

"Mr. Spencer, who do you think the two personages were?"

"Hold it, Elder Jackson! I know you want me to tell you they were Jesus Christ and God. But first, how do I know Joseph Smith saw *anything*? Or that there even *was* a Joseph Smith?"

Elder Jackson seemed unruffled by my objection. He moved smoothly along. "Mr. Spencer, I bear you my testimony, by the power of the Holy Ghost, that Joseph Smith did see God the Father and His Son, Jesus Christ, in the grove. And he saw them just as clearly as you can see Elder Morgan and me. And he could see that his own body truly was created in the image and likeness of God.

"Now at that time, the churches were teaching that God was only a spirit, that He had no body. But what do we learn about God from the experience of Joseph Smith?"

"You're still pushing, Elder. If Joseph Smith saw what you say he saw, then we would learn that God had a body."

"Right! Also, the churches taught that Jesus and the Father were the same being. But what does Joseph Smith's experience tell us about that?"

"Smith's vision, if true, would tell us that God the Father and Jesus Christ are two different beings."

"O.K., Mr. Spencer. Now I want to turn your attention to another matter." He pointed to the strip of paper on the flannel board. "From the Bible we learn that when Jesus Christ was on the earth, he established His Church, the Church of Jesus Christ. His followers were members of that Church. Here, let me read it from the Bible." He picked up his black leather Bible and thumbed through it.

"Here it is. Ephesians 2:19-20: 'Now therefore ye are no more strangers and foreigners, but fellow citizens with the saints, and of the household of God; and are built upon the foundation of the apostles and prophets, Jesus Christ himself being the chief corner stone.'"

Elder Jackson placed another strip of paper on the board that represented the foundation of a building. Written on it were the words *apostles* and *prophets*. "When Jesus Christ organized His own Church, it was called the Church of Jesus Christ. What were some of the officers He established in His organization?"

I sighed. I didn't appreciate being treated like a dunderhead, but I gave them the benefit of the doubt. Since they obviously followed a memorized program of dialogue, and probably talked to people of different levels of understanding, they had had to tailor their presentation to meet the needs of the most people.

"Apostles and prophets?" I said.

Another smile of approval. Elder Jackson was either a great actor or very simple.

"Mr. Spencer, as long as Jesus was on the earth, how many churches of Jesus Christ were there?"

"One."

"And even after Jesus died, with the foundation of the apostles and prophets, how many do you think there were?"

"One."

"That's right. There were not hundreds as there are today. The members of the Church of Jesus Christ all believed the same doctrine. And when the Church had a question or needed to know something, the people asked the apostles and prophets, who spoke for God. It makes sense, doesn't it?"

"Yes, I guess it does." I had to admit to myself that it *did* make sense.

"Mr. Spencer, you've used the word *if* a lot today. Let me ask you another 'if' question. If Jesus established His Church, and if He left it in the hands of men He appointed to keep it in order, then why are there hundreds of different churches today, with hundreds of different doctrinal ideas, each claiming to be a genuine Church of Christ?"

I was stumped. I could not give him an answer. Everything I thought of made no sense in the context of the present conversation. I was not a Bible student, and had only little knowledge of Christian doctrine. But I had to admit the things these young men were saying made sense. They knew where they were going. They knew what they believed. They were so *sure* of themselves.

"The reason for the confusion in the churches today," continued Elder Jackson, "is that after the death of Jesus the apostles were scattered. Eventually they were killed. The

Church, because of unbelief and wickedness, dwindled away. Which, I might add, is just what the Bible predicted would happen—that there would be a great falling away of the Church. We call it the Apostasy. The true Church did fall away and mankind plunged into the Dark Ages. It wasn't until 1820 that God found someone worthy enough to restore the Church through—the prophet Joseph Smith."

"Well, that's quite a story," I said.

"One last 'if' question. If what we have told you is true, what do you think the structure of the Church today should be like?"

"I guess it should be like the early Church."

"With apostles and prophets?"

"I suppose so."

"Do you know of any churches today that claim to be run by twelve apostles and a living prophet?"

"The Mormon Church?"

Jackson smiled. "If what we have told you is true, you'd want to be a member of the Mormon Church, wouldn't you?"

"Well, if it's true, I'd be a fool not to at least *consider* that."

Elder Jackson looked at Elder Morgan. He was ready. "Mr. Spencer," said the young man from Alabama in his slow, easy drawl, "I want to tell ya that I *know* what Eldah Jackson has said is true. I bear ya'll my own testimony that Joseph Smith was a true prophet of God, that this Church is God's True Church an' that we have a livin' prophet at the head of our Church today!"

Elder Jackson smiled at me as he began putting away his tripod and display board. "It's been really great for us to be with you today, Mr. Spencer."

"Yeah, well, it's been interesting. I can tell you really believe what you preach."

"We'd like to come back a week from today and talk to you again. Would morning or afternoon be better?" Glancing up at me, he smiled. "That is, if you want us to come back?"

I thought about my commitment to Lee. "Why not? Same time would be fine."

"One more thing, Mr. Spencer. We'd like to ask you to go to church with us next Sunday morning. It starts at ten."

"Oh, I don't know about that."

"Well, if you're going to take an honest look at the Church of Jesus Christ of Latter-day Saints, you really need to worship with us."

"I'm not sure that's necessary. Say, by the way, how did you come up with the name of your church?"

Elder Jackson looked glad I had asked. "Remember what Jesus called His Church?"

"The Church of Jesus Christ?"

"Right. When He restored the Church, He called it the same thing. But to distinguish the ancient Church from the Church today, we call ourselves the Church of Jesus Christ of *Latter-day Saints.* The word *saints* refers to anyone who is a member of Jesus' Church. So we are, as you can see, the Church of Jesus Christ of Latter-day Saints."

"Where does the name *Mormon* come from?"

"We're called Mormons because Joseph Smith translated gold plates he found buried in the ground that were written by a man named Mormon. And the book is called the Book of Mormon. We'll talk more about that next time."

"Sounds fair enough."

"Could we pick you up about 9:30 Sunday?"

"Oh, I suppose it wouldn't hurt to go *once.*"

As the two young men left, I pondered our conversation of the last hour. I liked them. They were everything I had never been—clean-cut, innocent, caught up in something

they believed in wholeheartedly. They left me some literature to read and promised to answer any questions I had at
our next meeting.

4

TAKING THE PLUNGE

Sunday morning dawned bright and clear. It was late August. It would be hot. As they promised, the missionaries arrived at 9:30. We rode to the church building on the east side of Santa Ana that they called "the ward." It was a brick structure—rambling, suggesting Spanish architecture—and quite plain.

Inside were wooden pews. The front of the church was elevated, where several people sat on pews. Three men sat in the center of the first row of pews behind the pulpit. The missionaries told me they were the bishop and his two counselors.

After we sang a couple hymns and heard several announcements, two boys, about twelve or fourteen years of age, prepared and blessed broken pieces of bread and small plastic cups of water. This, I was told, was the "sacrament." It was for members only.

After the sacrament, we went to a Sunday school class especially for those who, like myself, were investigating Mormonism. It was led by a fun-loving man who, I learned, was a chiropractor. All the people were friendly and went out of their way to greet me.

After Sunday school, during the fifteen-minute break before the next meeting, Elder Jackson discouraged me from slipping out to the parking lot and having a smoke. I agreed.

The next meeting started off just like the first one: opening hymns, announcements, and another round of sacrament. Then a man went to the podium to deliver the sermon. I was surprised that the bishop didn't address us, but Elder Morgan explained that the bishop seldom brought the message. Usually there was a special speaker chosen from the congregation, or sometimes from another ward. Once a month someone from the "stake" would come to speak. A stake was made up of about ten wards. All the leaders in the lower levels of the Church were laymen. That impressed me. *Religion of the people, by the people and for the people*, I thought.

The plainness of the building and the large number of noisy children disturbed me at first. Elder Jackson told me that Mormonism was a "family" religion. Everything centered around the family. Even the meetings were set up so that families could worship together. If that meant they were a little noisier than otherwise, it was worth it.

After the meetings, many people came up to shake my hand and welcome me. I felt important. More significantly, I felt loved—a sensation I did not often feel these days in my isolation at the gaming tables, or even in my ambitious womanizing.

One elderly gentleman introduced himself. "I'm Ed Ingles. I'm glad you were here today, son."

"I was glad to be here. I liked it."

"That's *wonderful!* There's nothing like the gospel, and being around God's people. Here, let me introduce my wife. Martha!" he called as he looked around behind him.

Martha was the ward mother. She gave me a big hug. Ed and Martha acted as proud of me as if I had been their own son. I appreciated the affection they showed me, and wondered if there wasn't buried deep inside me, going back to my parents' divorce or even farther, a boy's heart yearning for stability and a parent's love.

The next week the missionary-elders came back and we had our second meeting. We made an interesting threesome: the two young innocents with "sidewall" haircuts instructing the bearded skeptic.

The story they told in their missionary lessons was incredible. They talked about the fourteen-year-old boy, Joseph, who was directed by an angel to hidden gold plates that contained an account of the Lamanites, ancient inhabitants of North America, the forerunners of the American Indians. These Lamanites were supposedly visited by Jesus Himself during His life on earth. Joseph Smith translated the gold plates "by the gift and power of God" into the Book of Mormon.

We talked about the sworn testimony of the Three Witnesses, who said an angel appeared to them and showed them the gold plates and the writing upon them. And we discussed the sworn testimony of eight other witnesses who also claimed to have seen the gold plates of the Book of Mormon.

I tried to give the missionaries the benefit of the doubt, though the story they told me strained credulity. On the other hand, I was sick of bars and one-night stands and I needed something to believe in. My friendship with and respect for Lee was a powerful influence. He was so sure of himself, so sure he had found the answer.

Still, I hesitated to join the Church. I did not want to make any mistakes. Changing my entire lifestyle would be a big step and submitting myself to anyone, even these gentle folk, went against my grain. I struggled to be intellectually honest. But on a deeper level, I longed to be part of something decent.

As I hesitated, I continued to dialogue with Lee, who was growing impatient. "Jim," he said one night after we had talked for several hours, "you can go your own way, or you can go the right way, but you need to choose—now!"

Pressure was mounting for me to make a decision. Baptismal dates were suggested. The missionaries pointed out a passage in the Book of Mormon promising that, if I prayed sincerely, I would receive a witness from the Holy Spirit that the Church was true.

Every night I prayed, trying to come up with a feeling or sensation that would match what they told me to expect. I was torn. I wanted to be part of these people, but I wasn't sure about the Church.

It was clear, however, that they would not always be patient with me. I was expected to make a decision, and I felt it would be dishonest to join the Church if I did not really believe that Joseph Smith was a prophet and that the Book of Mormon was God's Word. I needed a sign—a sign that came during the fourth missionary lesson.

After seating ourselves in the living room, Elder Jackson began the discussion. They had already told me we would be talking about the "Word of Wisdom," which, they explained, was a prophecy brought by Joseph Smith forbidding the use of alcohol, tobacco, coffee and tea.

Elder Jackson opened his Bible. "Brother Spencer, John 8:31-32 tells us that as we come to know the truth, it will make us free. How do you think knowing the truth makes us free?"

"For one thing, it frees us from ignorance."

"Very good. Another way it frees us is from the punishment that comes from breaking God's natural laws. Gravity, for example, is a natural law. If we jump off a building, we break the law of gravity. And we pay a price, right?"

"Right!" I was learning that the best way to get along with Elder Jackson—which for some reason had become important to me—was to be as enthusiastic as he was. I still challenged him, but not on non-essentials.

"How do we know what God's laws are?"

"Through Scripture; through revelation."

"That's right. Through the Bible, the Book of Mormon, and other latter-day revelation. By the way, have you gotten an answer to your prayers yet about the Book of Mormon?"

"No, I haven't. But I'm still reading it every day and praying that God will show me if it is true."

"I'm sure that will happen if you continue to read and pray. Now, one of the revelations God has given us is the Word of Wisdom. In this revelation, the Lord told Joseph Smith that there are certain things men take into their bodies that harm them. And that if they continue to break this law of God they will pay a price, a physical price, in their bodies. Do you believe that is true?"

"Yes. I know I shouldn't smoke."

"What about drinking?"

"I haven't had a drink since I first started talking to you. Drinking is not a serious problem for me. I can take it or leave it. I'd rather take it, but I'm not hooked on it."

"Brother Spencer, what do you think about the commandment against the use of tobacco?"

"Well, I'm sure smoking is wrong. I'm not sure that God is too uptight about it, but I know it would be better if I didn't smoke."

Truth to tell, I was a little nervous about this line of questioning. I had been a chain-smoker for ten years and had tried many times to quit, but found it impossible. I was

hooked. Now I was getting the strong impression that Elder
Jackson was about to ask me to do the impossible.

"Brother Spencer, I want you to try to quit smoking."

"Wait a minute," I protested. "In the first place, I couldn't
quit if I wanted to. And in the second place, I don't know
that I want to!"

Elder Jackson was patient. "Look, brother, it's important
that you quit. Important to your physical health and important to your spiritual health. If you decide to join the
Church, it will be necessary for you to quit. All I'm asking
you to do is give it a try."

I was trapped. He was not going to give up. And, down
deep, I really wanted to be free of cigarettes. In exaspera-
tion, I took the package of Viceroys from my pocket and
flung it across the room. "O.K.," I exclaimed. "I don't think
I can quit and I'm not really sure I *want* to quit, but I'll try!"
They smiled at me and went on with the lesson.

After they left, I drove down to the Deseret Bookstore in
Orange and browsed through the Mormon books. Afterward, I stopped at a cafe for a soft drink. As I sat reading the
Book of Mormon, the most amazing truth dawned on me. I
had not had a cigarette—or wanted one—for two hours!

By that night I was sure something miraculous was in
motion. I *still* didn't want a cigarette.

Lee came over that night to see how I was doing. "It's a
miracle!" he exclaimed. "It's a sign from God. What more do
you need, man?"

I was convinced. Anything powerful enough to get me
off cigarettes had my attention. I was seeing the manifestation of some sort of spiritual power here—of what sort I was
not sure, but I *was* sure that I now wanted to join the
Mormon Church.

The missionaries were as elated as Lee. They quickly
finished off the last two lessons and interviewed me about

my personal life in preparation for baptism. I had already shaved my beard, which symbolized for me a new cleanness of life. Now I committed myself to be morally clean—extramarital sex was out of the question—and to abstain from alcohol, coffee and tea as well as tobacco.

I still could not bring myself to say, as Mormons are taught to say, that I knew Joseph Smith was a prophet, that the Book of Mormon was the Word of God, and that this was the True Church. But I was willing to say I *believed* it. And that was good enough. A baptismal date was selected.

The evening was warm and fresh. An afternoon rain had washed the city of Santa Ana for my baptism on September 27, 1964. Lee was there. I had never before seen him dressed in a suit. I myself entered the water dressed in a special white baptismal uniform.

Afterward, while I was seated in a chair, several elders—including Ed Ingles and the bishop—gathered around me, laid their hands on my head and confirmed me into the Church of Jesus Christ of Latter-day Saints. Later everybody stood around crying and hugging me. This time I knew I was really home. These people accepted me. I had become part of something wonderful!

When I was asked if I would like to say anything, I felt the desire to testify before everyone and share what was going on within me. I planned to say that I believed the Church to be true, Joseph Smith to be a prophet, and the Book of Mormon to be the Word of God.

But when I stood to speak, I heard myself saying, "I *know* that Joseph Smith was a prophet. I *know* the book of Mormon is the Word of God. I *know* this is God's True Church and that it is headed by a living prophet today."

And I did know it! I had come to know it. I had, by some amazing power, become a True Believer like the others.

Now nothing stood in my way for full fellowship and acceptance into the Kingdom of God and into His True Church.

5

A TRUE BELIEVER

No one, it is said, is more zealous than a convert. When I finally made the decision to join the Mormon Church, I jumped in with both feet. By this time I was living in my own apartment in Santa Ana and still working in electronics. Now I immersed myself in the life and activity of the Church.

Lee, of course, was a great support and encouragement. Angela was not as impressed. In fact, she wanted nothing to do with "weird religious stuff." Finally I abandoned trying to talk to her and eventually stopped calling her altogether.

Actually, my new commitment to Mormonism forced me to reevaluate all my friendships. One afternoon, for example, two old Navy friends stopped by for a drink since they were in town. One of them, Ken, had been my closest friend next to Lee and Fred Johnson; and I had stood up for the other one, Les, in his wedding. I was delighted to see both of them.

But when we drove down to a local bar and I ordered orange juice, they stopped me up short.

"Orange juice?" exclaimed Ken, sitting next to me in the booth. "What's the matter, Jim? You sick?"

"Ah, well, no . . . not exactly. The truth is, I quit drinking."

Ken laughed. Then he looked me in the eye. "You're not kidding."

"No," I smiled. "I'm not."

Les looked up from across the booth and whistled. "Now *this* is an event. Jim Spencer quit drinking!"

I laughed. "So, what's new in your lives? I haven't seen you, Les, for two years."

"Just a minute," said Ken. "I want to know why you aren't having a drink with us."

"I hardly know how to tell you this. I—well, I've joined the Mormon Church."

"Give me a break," said Les. "You *what?* I don't believe it. This is one of your practical jokes."

"No," said Ken, still looking at me. "He's not kidding."

I looked down at my orange juice. "No, I'm not."

"I guess I'm not surprised," he said. "Underneath it all, you always have been a religious critter. I'm a little sorry. But on the other hand, I respect your position. Sometime, not now, I'd like to hear about it."

"Sometime I'd like to talk to you about it."

The conversation turned to old times. Nothing more was said about my orange juice. But the conversation was abbreviated. After an hour Les looked at his watch, made an excuse and said they really needed to get going. I said I understood.

And I did understand. As we separated, I understood that nothing would ever be the same. And I doubted somehow that I would see either one of them again.

I threw myself into Mormonism with zeal. In Mor-

monism, activity is the mark of faithfulness. *Is he active?* is
the question most often asked to determine if a person is a
"good" Mormon. Does he obey the dictates of the Church
by adhering to the Word of Wisdom—the prohibition of
coffee and tea, as well as alcohol and tobacco?

As a faithful Mormon, I willingly gave ten percent of all
my earnings to the Church. Every year the bishop had a
"tithing settlement" with each family in the ward. If they
gave a full ten percent they were known as "full tithers."

Tremendous emphasis was placed on attendance at meetings. Sunday mornings, for me, started with a priesthood
meeting at 7 a.m., followed by Sunday school at nine. I was
back at the ward by 4:30 for a sacrament meeting. On
Sunday evenings I often attended a "Fireside"—a special
gathering for a lecture or slide presentation.

A group of single adults met together on Monday nights
for Family Home Evening. We would sing songs, follow a
lesson outline prepared by Church leadership in Salt Lake
City and have refreshments. The same kind of gathering
was held every Monday night in every good Latter-day
Saint home.

On Wednesday nights the Mutual Improvement Association (M.I.A.) met for study groups and activities designed
to make us better Mormons and better citizens. Tuesday
and Thursday nights we often had leadership meetings for
auxiliaries such as Sunday school or M.I.A.

Saturday mornings were priesthood leadership meetings. Also on Saturdays there would be special work proj-
ects at the stake farm or perhaps maintenance on the ward
building. And Friday or Saturday nights you could count on
some special program on a ward or stake level.

Of course, there was always temple work for those who
held Temple Recommends—a privilege awarded to the
small percentage of Mormon membership considered

worthy to go through the temple. And since no one could go to heaven who had not gone through the temple, we were encouraged to do genealogy research, in order that our forbears could go through the temple "by proxy" through a living Church member.

The Church considered "every member a missionary." We were expected to make contacts for the missionaries and plot how to get our neighbors to church. The important thing was to keep busy!

My own zeal did not go unnoticed. I was soon ordained through all the offices of the Lesser (Aaronic) Priesthood. And I was called to be a member of the Sunday school superintendency. After a year I was ordained into the Higher (Melchizedek) Priesthood as an elder.

Meanwhile I was making new friends. Ed Ingles became my spiritual mentor. I spent much time at the Ingles' home, having dinner with them after church on Sundays and dropping by to chat in the evenings when nothing was going on at the ward. Ed and Martha took me in as a son. I loved them dearly.

Ed was the one I turned to whenever I had a question about the faith or when there was something I did not understand. Once I asked him why the Book of Mormon was written in Elizabethan English. Joseph Smith had translated it from "Reformed Egyptian" into English, yet it was not written in the English of Joseph Smith's day, but in an older, seventeenth-century style. Ed explained to me that it was written in King James English because it would be better received by the people if it sounded like the Bible.

One warm summer evening I went over to the Ingles' with a big concern I wanted to talk to Ed about. I had been driving down a boulevard lined with orange trees in Tustin, California, when I spotted a church building off the road. I could barely make out the words *Church of Jesus Christ of*

Latter-day Saints on a sign, but something was wrong with the building. I had never seen a frame Mormon church building; they were all brick. When I turned my car into the parking lot for a closer look, I saw an unfamiliar word in the title: *Reorganized.* The *Reorganized* Church of Jesus Christ of Latter-day Saints!

"What's this?" I wondered aloud. As I watched people enter the church building, the idea of dissension within the Church sent a chill of fear through me. After all, it was in part the disunity within Christendom that had drawn me into the true, restored Church. I decided to ask Ed about this unnerving development.

In the Ingles' living room, Ed leaned back in his over-stuffed study chair and listened patiently as I explained what I had seen and the effect it had had on me. "What do you know about the Reorganized Church?" I asked at last.

Ed laughed disarmingly. "I understand how you must feel, son. It must be kind of a shock to realize there are those not of the Lord's Church who call themselves Latter-day Saints. But don't worry about the Reorganites. They're just a group of malcontents who broke away from the Church long ago. It's a tiny group. They're in deception. Forget it, son. It's nothing."

"But I don't understand. How can anyone who once knew the truth fall away?"

"Just forget about it, Jim. It's one of those black marks in the history of the Church. They have nothing of value to say."

"But how can they even use the name of the Church?"

Ed's smile faded. "They're apostates, son. They're losers!" His face became uncharacteristically hard. He added grimly, "Stay away from them!"

As I saw his determination, something melted within me. My fear faded. In its place came a new determination—

one based on trust, submitting itself confidently to the man of God who sat before me. I saw in Ed's eyes the fire of the prophet.

Who were these Reorganites, anyway? I asked myself. *How dare they stand against the Lord's Church?* I felt pity and revulsion for them.

Ed came to my rescue another time one Sunday after church. I had been disturbed by an incident in the early morning priesthood meeting. The priesthood teacher had mentioned in passing a concept he called Eternal Progression. He said that God had once been a man and had *progressed* to godhood! I found that impossible to believe and protested, saying it was blasphemous to talk about God having once been a man.

Over dinner at Ed's I brought up the subject, telling what the teacher had said and my response.

"He was telling you the truth," said Ed, not looking up from the roast beef he was carving.

"But Brother Ingles," I protested, "God is God and man is man. How can it be said that God was once a man?"

"Well, Jim, there are a lot of things you don't understand now that you will understand later. The prophet Joseph did teach that God is an exalted man. What he actually said was, 'As man is, God once was; as God is, man may become.' He told us that God is an exalted man, who was once as we are now."

I was irritated. "I don't understand how—"

"Well, son," Ed interrupted, "if you'll listen maybe you will!"

"I'm sorry, sir. It's just such a strange thought. I mean, I've always thought that God was always God."

Ed smiled at me again. I felt relieved to know he wasn't angry.

"The fact is, Jim, God progressed to godhood. He *was* a man. He had a father. He became a god through obedience to the laws and ordinances of the universe. Now, I know that's hard to understand when you first hear it. But you'll come in good time to understand that truth, as well as many other things you cannot receive now."

I knew he was referring to things I would learn in the temple—if and when I was worthy to enter that sacred place.

"I'll tell you one more thing you might as well know. It's a wonderful truth that will thrill you when you finally come to understand and accept it. It is not only true that God became God, but it is also true that His doing so was not unusual."

"What do you mean?"

"I mean that He is not the only being to have so progressed."

"You mean there are other—other beings that—other gods?"

"That's exactly what I mean."

My heart sank. I did not like what I was hearing.

"Not only that, my dear boy, but there are others who have become gods, and still others who will become gods!"

"You mean other *men*."

"Precisely."

I was shocked and confused. I had been a member of the Church only a few months. I knew there were lots of things I had to learn. I knew there were temple ordinances that were yet to be revealed to me. These, Ed had said, were not *secret*, but they were *sacred*, so they were not discussed outside the walls of the temple.

But I had not thought there would be anything so grand in scope as this to be learned. What I was hearing challenged the deepest recesses of my soul. Something in me rebelled at the words, resisting the thought that God had not always been God.

"Joseph Smith said that God was not God from all eternity," Ed was saying, "but that He learned to become a god. And that we, too, must learn to become gods."

"But I don't want to learn to become a god," I objected weakly.

Ed laughed. Smiling at Martha across the table, he got up and walked toward the kitchen. "How about a root beer, son?"

My stomach felt lined with lead. I was reeling from what I was hearing. But the Church was the final authority on matters of conduct and doctrine, and I believed that the Church was founded by God Himself. It was the restored Church. Christianity had gone completely wrong. The Church was headed by a living prophet, David O. McKay, who communed personally with God. Who was I to contest the prophets? To trust my own feeble understanding, or to question the Church?

And I knew that to question the Church would separate me from my people, my religion and everything important to me. I had heard stories of those who questioned too much. They could not receive the truth. They were rebellious. They would eventually separate themselves from God's Church and become apostate!

I could not bear to think of losing the acceptance and approval of my new friends, as well as the Church. I was not ready to pit my own understanding against that of the brotherhood. When in doubt, I was told, trust the leaders of the Church. God would never let the prophets fall. I had to keep my eyes on the Church. The alternative was to set myself up as one who had greater insight and understanding than God's anointed leaders: the first step on the slippery path to apostasy.

I had a decision to make. I could either trust my own understanding or commit myself deeper to the Church, and to all the things that were good—Family Home Evening, home teaching, Sunday school, priesthood meetings, sacrament meetings, not to mention all my friends. All these were such a far cry from the licentiousness and wickedness of my life before the Church that I was overwhelmed with gratitude.

Ed stood silhouetted in the doorway, arms akimbo. Because of the light streaming in from the kitchen behind him, I could not see his face, but I knew he was watching me intently. Would I continue to argue, or would I accept what he was saying?

I found my voice. "I'll have a root beer, Ed."

"Good boy!" Ed exclaimed. "Good boy. You're going to be an asset to the Kingdom, son!"

6

ENTANGLING RELATIONSHIPS

More and more my life centered in the activities of the Church. When I wasn't working, I was studying Church doctrine or fellowshiping with Church members. It was wonderful. God's people loved and accepted me, and I worked hard to be worthy of the confidence the leadership placed in me.

One evening I arrived home from work to a ringing telephone. Bishop Satterfield wanted me to come over to his office after dinner.

As I drove to the church, I wondered what the bishop could want. I was already a counselor in the Sunday school superintendency and I couldn't think of another position he might want me to serve in. As I pulled into the driveway, I could see the light on in Bishop Satterfield's office.

Inside, the bishop looked up from a sheaf of papers on his desk, rose, smiled and took my hand. He was about 35, short, with glossy black hair and a winsome personality.

"Thank you so much for coming over," he said warmly.

"My pleasure, Bishop."

"Jim, I'll come right to the point. We've been watching your progress in the gospel. We are very pleased with you."

I glowed with pride. "Thank you very much. I just want to serve!"

"We see that, Jim. And we want you to have the opportunity to do just that. You have been serving in the Sunday school superintendency for nearly a year now, haven't you?"

"Yes, that's right. And I love it!"

"You certainly have the respect of the teachers and the children. That's the only thing that holds me back from what I am about to ask of you. What would you think about giving up that job?"

"Well, Bishop, of course I'll do whatever you tell me."

"I was sure you'd say that. Before I talk to you about another calling, I need to ask you a few questions. I think I already know the answers, but it's necessary for me to ask you these things formally."

"Sure. Go ahead."

"You, of course, are a full tither?"

"Yes, sir."

"And you are living the Word of Wisdom?"

"Yes, I am."

"I know you are faithful in attendance at meetings, because I observe that. Do you believe that David O. McKay is a true prophet of God?"

"I do."

"And are you morally clean? I know you date. Are you compromising in any way the standards of sexual purity of the Church?"

"No, sir. I am morally clean."

"As I said, I was sure of the questions before I asked you. Jim, we would like you to serve a stake mission for the Church."

I don't think anything he could have said would have surprised or delighted me more. A stake mission was similar to a full-time mission call (such as that of Elder Jackson and Elder Morgan), except that it was limited to forty hours per month of service, plus it was local, performed within the boundaries of the local stake. Aside from that, the work was exactly the same. It was a position of real responsibility.

"We don't want you to give us your answer tonight, Jim," continued the bishop. "Pray about it and let me know your decision within the next week or ten days."

Outside in the parking lot, I sprinted to my car. I was exhilarated. To be called to a mission after only one year in the Church! I was humbled by the thought. Even more wonderful, I realized that if I were to serve a mission, I would have to go through the temple! Obviously the bishop had thought of that.

Going through the temple, that privilege reserved for the most faithful in the Church, had been my highest goal. I already knew what my decision would be. I would tell the bishop that I would certainly be a stake missionary.

It was a big night. We were having a men's meeting on the eve of General Conference, a semi-annual convocation in Salt Lake City. Our meeting was attended by men from three stakes who came together at the Orange Stake Center. I was to hear the voice of the living prophet live via special telephone hookup.

One of the things that most impressed me about the Church, which Elder Jackson had told me about on my first visit to the ward, was its emphasis on family life. I was especially impressed by the commitment and sacrifice I saw fathers exhibit for their families, particularly since my own parents had divorced and I had been denied a close relationship with my father. The Church recognized the father as the head of his house, just as men were to lead and govern the Church. The General Authorities—the upper-level management in Salt Lake City—were all elderly patriarchs who led the Church with uncompromising strength.

This particular night, I watched men sitting reverently in the auditorium of the Stake Center with their arms draped over the shoulders of their sons. I envied that relationship, and recognized how fortunate I was to be a part of such a wonderful organization.

Suddenly, over the speakers in the room came the voice of David O. McKay, prophet, seer and revelator of the four-million-member Church of Jesus Christ of Latter-day Saints. As President McKay began to speak, something startling happened: All the men in the room stood to their feet singing "We Thank Thee, O God, for a Prophet." I had sung the hymn many times in sacrament meeting. I loved it, as I loved the hymn we sang about Joseph Smith, "Praise to the Man!" It was an emotional moment. Many in the room wept.

Then President McKay, his 90-year-old voice quavering with emotion, begged us to be true to our God, our families and our Church. At the end of his speech, we again stood to our feet in song.

After the meeting I drove around Santa Ana reflecting on the evening. I had a hard time going to sleep that night. What a privilege to be a young Mormon missionary!

Since the Mormon Church places high emphasis on family life, young people are encouraged to marry young and have lots of children. For that reason, the Church provides opportunities for young people to meet in healthy social situations. Family Home Evening on Monday nights provided just such an opportunity, when we single adults were encouraged to meet together and have our own fellowship time. The Mutual Improvement Association organized dances, parties and co-educational softball games. Every Sunday night after church we went out for dessert or soft drinks.

One group of girls shared an apartment and often invited the single men over for dinner on Sunday afternoons. After dinner we played the guitar, sang and watched television.

One afternoon a new girl showed up for dinner. She was beautiful, with long black hair and dark eyes. She was also vivacious, with a good sense of humor, and I was attracted to her immediately. After dinner, I taught her some songs. She had a beautiful trained voice. I wanted to ask her out, yet because I was so involved in my mission I didn't want any entangling relationships. So I decided just to be her friend. That seemed to suit her.

But after a month or so of exchanging pleasantries at church and church social gatherings, I noticed that a couple of the other young men were asking her out and she was accepting. That motivated me to ask her for a date.

We took a long drive from Santa Ana to Riverside and back. We talked about our personal hopes and dreams, but mostly about our lives as they related to the Church. She was from a good Mormon family and the Church was very important to her.

I was captivated. What I noticed most was that she was the most honest person I had ever met. She was guileless. By the time I dropped her off at her apartment in Santa Ana, I knew I had a problem. And its name was Margaretta.

The Los Angeles Temple sits like a jewel atop a beautifully manicured hillside in the heart of Los Angeles. The night of January 15, 1966, I entered the building for the first time. I made my way down a corridor to the basement in a company of dozens of others coming for the 7:00 p.m. session.

In my pocket was a Temple Recommend, the official document signed by my bishop and my stake president. They had interviewed me and found me worthy to enter the house of the Lord. In addition to answering the questions the bishop had already asked me, I had sworn that I upheld the General Authorities of the Church and that I was not in sympathy or in any way connected with apostate groups.

At a checkpoint, a temple worker took my Recommend, examined it and stamped it. At a window I rented white clothing—shirt, pants, belt, socks and shoes. I also picked special temple clothing.

I was then directed to a dressing room, where I removed my clothes and placed them in a locker. I put on a garment called a "shield"—a piece of white cotton cloth with a hole for the head. The garment hung down the front and back of my body with the sides open.

I walked into a booth in the Washing and Anointing Room where a temple worker recited the ritual of washing—that I would "be free from the blood and sins of this generation"—as he dipped his right hand in water, reached under the shield and touched various parts of my body. He ritualistically washed my head, "that my brain and intellect would be clear and active." He washed my ears, eyes, nose, lips, neck, shoulders, chest, arms and hands, abdomen, and then my legs and feet. The same process was repeated with oil in an anointing ceremony.

Next I was handed a special temple garment, which I was told represented the garment God gave Adam in the Garden of Eden. This garment, unless I defiled it, would be "a shield and protection for me against the power of the De-

stroyer until I finished my work on earth." From this day
on, I was to wear such a temple garment, in place of ordi-
nary underwear, for the rest of my life.

Then I went back to my locker and put it on, along with
the white outer clothing I had rented. I carried with me the
other clothing, which I was told I would put on later in the
ceremony.

Then I was given a new name which I was never to reveal
to anyone, except at a designated place in the temple ceremony. Now I was ready for the Creation Room.

In that room a temple worker told us we would watch a
play reenacting the creation of the world. In it we would
hear the voices of Elohim, Jehovah and Michael the arch-
angel. (I knew Elohim to be the father of Jehovah, who was
actually Jesus Christ.) In the play, the three heavenly beings
organized the earth: they divided the light and darkness,
and they created vegetation, animals, and eventually Adam
and Eve. Also in the Creation Room I swore an oath, along
with about a hundred others, to sacrifice everything I had,
including my life, for the Church.

The next part of the ceremony left me a little bewildered.
Terms were introduced which I did not understand. The
character representing Elohim, or God, addressed us. He
had previously led us in the oath of sacrifice. He now told us
he was required to give us "the First Token of the Aaronic
Priesthood," along with its *name, sign* and *penalty*. He impressed us that what he was about to reveal to us was very
sacred and that we must promise never to reveal it to
anyone, under any condition, even at the peril of our lives.

The *Token* was a secret handshake, which he showed to
us.

The *name* of the Token, he said, was the secret new name
we had received earlier in the temple ceremony.

The *sign* of the Token was made by placing our right

thumb under our left ear, with our palms open flat and down.

The *penalty,* Elohim said, was a representation of the way a life could be taken. The penalty for revealing this first Token was depicted by drawing our thumbs "quickly across the throat to the right ear."

By this time I was growing most uncomfortable. I felt something was wrong. One of the things I had liked most about Mormonism was the simplicity of its church services. I liked the inornate settings and the plain, frank people. I now found myself in a ceremony I didn't like at all. *What was wrong with me?* Ed had promised me that this would be the greatest day of my life; that he had his most spiritual experiences at the temple.

As I brooded about this, the temple worker moved us into the next room, which he called the Lone and Dreary World.

In the Lone and Dreary World another play was enacted. A man playing the part of Lucifer had a dialogue with a man representing Adam. Lucifer introduced to Adam a man dressed in black who represented a preacher. To the preacher Lucifer said, "I will give you five thousand dollars to preach to this man." The preacher held out for more money since it had cost him so much to go to college to learn how to preach. Lucifer promised to raise his pay if he did well.

Then the preacher said to Adam, "Good morning, sir. Do you believe in a God who is without body, parts or passions; who sits on top of a topless throne; whose center is everywhere and whose circumference is nowhere; who fills the universe, yet is so small He can dwell within your heart?"

Adam replied that he could not comprehend such a Being.

"That's the beauty of it!" the preacher replied. "Perhaps you believe in hell, that great bottomless pit which is full of fire and brimstone, into which the wicked are cast and where they are continually burning and yet are never consumed?"

Adam said he couldn't believe in that, either.

After more dialogue, seemingly designed to make the preacher look foolish, the play was interrupted and we were instructed to put on the additional articles of clothing we had been carrying. They included a sash—called a robe—a white cloth cap, and a green apron embroidered with fig leaves. We then were given another secret handshake with its name, sign and penalty. This time the name was my own first name, and the penalty, disembowelment.

The rest of the evening offered a continuation of the same plays, oaths, Tokens, signs and penalties. We went through the Terrestrial World, the Law of Chastity, the First Token of the Melchizedek Priesthood (or Sign of the Nail), the Law of Consecration, the Second Token of the Melchizedek Priesthood (the Patriarchal Grip or Sure Sign of the Nail).

Finally we went Through the Veil where we stood on one side of a curtain separating the Terrestrial World from the Celestial World and gave the Tokens and their names to a worker who stood on the other side of the veil. The handshakes took place through a hole in the veil. After we had (with much prompting) said all the right things and given all the right signs, we were admitted into a beautifully furnished Celestial Room, and the ceremony was over.

I drove home in paralyzed shock and wonder. I had absolutely no comprehension what had happened in the temple. It made no sense to me. It repulsed me and angered me. Yet working against all those fears was the thought that I was in no position to tell the Church, the eldership, the General Authorities or God what to do. I did not understand. I must be wrong. It was as simple as that. In the morning I would wake up and understand. Now I just wanted to go home and go to bed and go to sleep.

In the morning, however, I felt no better. I stewed over the thing. I considered going to see Ed, but I wasn't up to facing him with such an issue. I thought I was losing my mind. I had just completed what was supposed to be the most wonderful spiritual event of my life, the event that would open up new vistas for my spiritual development, and I felt drained. *What in the world had gone on in there?*

I knew I had to talk to Ed.

"I know exactly how you feel, son. I felt the same way myself the first time I went through the temple. It is such a spiritual experience! Everything is so different from the way things happen in the outside world that you feel disoriented and confused."

"That's exactly how I feel!"

"Jim, I could tell you all kinds of things. I could tell you that the temple ceremony is the most wonderful thing God has revealed to man—which, by the way, it is. But that would only make you more confused. You can't lean on my testimony here. You must find this out for yourself."

"But how am I going to do that?"

"There is only one way to do that."

"What is it? Tell me!"

"You have to go back and go through the ceremony again. Go back every week if you have to. Go back at least seven times. I have gone hundreds. I guarantee you that if you'll go back seven times and really pray, God will show you the secrets of the temple."

I left Ed's determined to do what he had told me. And I did: I went back for the next seven Friday nights. The only thing different was that, since the temple also exists for the dead who did not go through while alive, I went through on behalf of people who had died. Each time, I was given a slip of paper with some name on it—one like Henry Cook, Richard Dewes, Henry Barton, Jacob Holden, Paul Moseley—supplied by a Church member from personal genealogical research. And I went through the washings, anointings, oaths, Tokens, signs and penalties in proxy for that deceased person.

I still did not feel completely comfortable with the temple ceremony. It seemed alien to the simplicity of the Church. But I felt angry with myself for not feeling differently. Obviously I was not as spiritual as the bishop thought.

After worrying for nearly two months about my inability to appreciate the temple ceremony, I decided the only way to handle it was to try to put it out of my mind. The temple concept was apparently bigger and deeper than I was able to comprehend. There was no sense letting it disturb me. After all, the leadership of the Church knew what was best. Someday I would understand.

In the interim, though I would still go to the temple from time to time, I decided to absorb myself in activity and continue to serve the Church.

Margaretta and I had begun to date regularly. My plan to avoid entangling relationships was failing. I was falling in love with her. One day I asked her if she would like to go with me to visit a family Lee and I had met in Mexico.

We crossed the border at Mexicali and drove a hundred miles down the Baja to San Felipe on the Gulf of California. There my friend Antonio earned his living as part of a cooperative that fished for shark. We spent the weekend helping him—riding far out into the Gulf to tend the nets, pulling sharks into the old fifteen-foot whaleboat, getting sick from the blood and the rolling of the boat in the swells of the warm Gulf water.

In the early evening twilight we walked the beach. Margaretta knew what I was going to ask her.

"I want to take you to the temple."

"I know."

"Well, what do you think?"

"I don't know."

"Yes, but what do you *think?*"

"I need some time. It's a big decision."

"Would it help if I told you I can't live without you?"

"I'm afraid not."

"O.K., then I won't say that."

But before our trip to Mexico was over, she told me she would marry me.

We made plans for an October wedding. Coincidentally, Lee had moved back to Wyoming, met a girl and was making plans of his own. So we decided to make it a double wedding in the Idaho Falls Temple.

Margaretta looked lovely in her long white gown. We knelt on satin pillows across a white altar. Mirrors on both walls reflected and re-reflected our images into infinity, representing that our marriage was "for time and all eternity."

I felt happier than I ever thought possible.

As a young married man, I moved to an even deeper level of commitment to the Church. The bishop released me from my mission, saying it would not be right for me to spend so much time away from home as a newlywed.

Soon Margaretta was pregnant. Within a year our baby daughter, Erin, was born. I was overwhelmed by the round, pink, trusting bundle, gazing confidently into the eyes of her father, Elder Spencer, Mormon leader, True Believer.

It was time to move even deeper.

Since the Mormon Church encourages excellence, it places a strong emphasis on education. And now that decency and order were part of my life, it was natural that I should turn my attention to preparing for maximum usefulness in the Church. That meant college. Margaretta agreed to continue working and we would take advantage of the educational benefits of the G.I. Bill, since I was a veteran.

So I was accepted at Ricks College in Rexburg, Idaho, just twelve miles from the town of St. Anthony, where Margaretta grew up and where her parents still lived.

We headed for college full of hope and enthusiasm. Surely God was good to us and we were being led by Him. We had no idea that Ricks would become a junction in the road on our spiritual journey.

7

THE DOUBTS BEGIN

It was New Year's Day, 1969, and the snow crunched under the tires as I drove into St. Anthony, Idaho. I had packed all our possessions into a U-Haul trailer. Nestled among pillows and clothing in the back seat of the car lay my one-year-old daughter, Erin. The front seat was occupied by me and a caged parakeet. Margaretta would follow by plane two weeks later.

We rented a small apartment in St. Anthony. Margaretta got a job at a local bank a block from the apartment and I commuted to school in nearby Rexburg.

We had no furniture, but Margaretta's folks provided some used things and bought us a good mattress, which we laid on the floor of the only bedroom. As we unpacked, Margaretta looked around and frowned. "Where are we going to put Erin's crib? There isn't enough room in our bedroom."

"How about in here?" I called from the depths of a large closet opening off the living room. The closet turned out to be a fine bedroom. There was even enough room left over for storage.

Eating our first supper together in the little kitchen that night, I looked across the table at Margaretta. "Well, kid, what do you think? Are you glad to be back in your home-town?"

"I really am. I like it here. And how do things look at school?"

"I've taken a really full load. I didn't realize it's been nearly ten years since I went to school. It'll be a challenge."

"You can handle it."

"Did you know I was on probation?"

"What for?"

"Because I was a high school dropout, and only got my diploma by taking those correspondence courses. So when I registered they said I'd be on probation the entire first semester. I have to get good marks."

"You can do it."

"I'm worried about my Spanish class."

"Why?"

"I'm taking second-year Spanish."

"Good grief! Why?"

"I told the professor I'd spent a lot of time in Mexico and could speak the language pretty well."

"Man, was that dumb!"

"What do you mean?" I replied indignantly. "I *have* spent a lot of time in Mexico. I can speak enough Spanish to get by!"

"Listen, buddy, I was with you in Mexico. You couldn't order a taco from a street vendor."

"Give me a break!"

She was laughing. She came over and sat on my lap. "The last thing you need is a break. My job is to keep you from getting a big head."

"Well, you're a real success," I said sullenly. But I looked up at her sparkling black eyes and laughed. I shoved her off onto the floor and began tickling her.

Ricks College overlooks the farming community of Rexburg from a hill marking the boundary of the Snake River flood plain, which stretches like a flat ribbon across the state. Rexburg is part of a group of communities that form the center of the famous Idaho potato industry. The people of the Upper Snake River Valley are hard-working, prosperous, politically conservative and dedicated to the Mormon Church. Mormon parents send their children from throughout the United States to the two-year college in Rexburg, knowing they will be safe from drugs, crime and revolutionary ideas.

With college campuses in revolt during the 1960s, I felt privileged to be accepted at Ricks. Here things were safe and secure. Bright-eyed, moderately dressed students scurried across the campus like bees in the Deseret hive. The most radical activity I observed was that of students violating the *Keep Off the Grass* signs.

Although I had been placed on probation, the classwork proved easy, and after the first semester I was an honor student with a scholarship. But before long I began to wonder if the college atmosphere was a little *too* secure. In an attempt to avoid the liberal extremes of college life, the philosophy at Ricks promoted conformity at the expense of intellectual excellence.

The fact that I was nearly ten years older than most of the students, who were freshly graduated from high school, made things even more difficult. I soon found that I had more in common with the teachers than the students. I became close friends with one of my professors. We played chess together during lunch break. With our wives, we double-dated to the movies and got together for dinner.

Bill Fredericks and I saw many of the same problems at Ricks. We decried the provincialism and isolation as a head-in-the-sand approach to real life. We longed for expanded thinking and discussion and, yes, even debate on relevant issues of the day. Neither Bill nor I connected the problems at school with problems within the Church. "The Church is perfect," we would say to each other. "It is the people who are imperfect."

I was surprised at the tactics used to enforce discipline on campus. Students who lived on campus gave up certain civil liberties. Campus police could, for example, conduct unannounced room searches at any time, day or night. And campus dress codes were extremely strict, not only forbidding long hair on male students, but also requiring them to be clean-shaven. Despite Mormonism's hairy-faced founders like Brigham Young, even a mustache meant expulsion from school.

The town of Rexburg had been founded by a Mormon polygamist named Ricks. More than ninety percent of the 10,000 townspeople were Mormon. Rugged individualism was the cornerstone of the community. Conservative third-party candidates were welcomed here. Polling places were located according to Church ward boundaries. A volunteer posse was organized among the Mormon faithful, which the county sheriff fearfully called a vigilante group. Many neighboring towns, rather than hold parades on the Fourth of July, elected instead to celebrate July 24, the anniversary of Brigham Young's entrance to the Salt Lake Valley.

During my stay at Ricks, the nation was agonizing over the Vietnam War. Hippies and protest marches dominated headlines. But never was there a march or demonstration at

Ricks College. In fact, there was never even a public discussion of the war.

I myself was far from radical: I was a veteran, family man and loyal, committed Mormon. But I believed that part of the responsibility of an institution of higher learning, religious or secular, was to challenge young people intellectually and present a balanced view of current events.

So the intellectual paralysis on campus began to trouble me. Ricks College seemed to be in the business of producing men and women who were unquestioningly dedicated not only to the moral but also the political and social values of the Mormon Church.

The Church's position regarding blacks became a particular trouble spot in my thinking. In the 1960s blacks could not hold the priesthood. According to the Church, blacks were descended from Ham, the son of Noah, and under a curse. Brigham Young had said that blacks would never hold the priesthood.

It shamed me that many of my Mormon friends used the Church to support their racial prejudices. They liked to point to the story in the Book of Mormon in which dark-skinned Lamanites turned "white and delightsome"[1] when they believed the gospel message. I myself was not racially prejudiced and had a hard time believing God was. But I was forced to submit to the Church's position regarding blacks. After reading all I could by Church leaders on the subject, I was finally forced to relegate one more troubling issue to the back of my mind. The Church, being infallible, must have the understanding I lacked.

---

[1] Since then, Mormon prophet Spencer W. Kimball received a revelation granting priesthood to blacks. Subsequently, the Book of Mormon was changed. New editions say the Lamanites became *"pure* and delightsome" (italics mine).

In my last months at Ricks, I witnessed a series of events that revealed deep-seated problems.

One incident had its roots in a conflict among Mormons regarding the Word of Wisdom, which prohibits, among other things, "hot drinks." All Mormons agree that this includes coffee and tea, but the most conservative Mormons believe it also includes soft drinks containing caffeine—for example, cola drinks.

The official college position was anti-cola. There were numerous soft drink machines on campus, but none contained cola—only root beer, lemon-lime, grape and orange.

As an older and privileged student, I had contacts with the faculty and was invited into the faculty lounges to play chess with the teachers. I discovered that all the faculty lounges had Coca-Cola in them. In fact, some of the lounges were literally stacked with cases of Coke.

To my knowledge, it never occurred to anyone to question the procedure. Everyone knew that the president of the college had decreed that there be no cola on campus. The entire faculty and staff knew that the lounges were full of Coke. The students brought in their own supply. Yet no one seemed to think anything was amiss.

By this time I was a staff member of the college newspaper and wrote a weekly editorial column. Often in the column I would point out contradictions in college life. In time, the column began to be viewed as controversial.

One day, while playing chess with Bill and sipping a Coke, I suddenly realized how silly it was for two grown men to sneak around hiding soft drinks.

"Bill," I asked as I watched him capture my king's rook, "what would you think of a column called 'The Great Coke Cover-Up'?"

"Not much," he replied absently. Then, sensing I was

serious, he looked up. "Really, Jim, I do *not* think that would be wise."

"Why not?"

"Because all I think you would do is infuriate the administration."

"Yeah, but the position is dumb. Here we are telling everybody you shouldn't drink Coke. And here we sit, drinking the stuff ourselves."

"I know."

"I mean, we need to either get the stuff off campus or put in Coke machines. And since one hundred percent of the students and ninety-eight percent of the faculty drink Coke, I think the latter course would be more reasonable."

"Jim, there's no use talking about it. It's an area that cannot be discussed."

"*Any* area can be discussed!"

"Not here. You're in check, by the way."

But I had lost interest in the game. "Come on, Bill, help me write an editorial."

"Not on your life."

"Chicken."

"Squawk!"

I sighed. "O.K., I'll have to do it on my own."

Bill stared at me. He could see my mind was made up. He got up, picked up a manila folder and headed for the door. "I have a class in ten minutes. Since you choose to be obstinate and recalcitrant, I am leaving early."

"See you tomorrow for lunch," I said.

What a nervous Nelly, I thought as he closed the door. *How could anyone get that upset about a story that's factual?*

When the paper came out the following week, I found out that Bill had a better understanding of the climate on campus than I did. The hue and cry that went up from the faculty astonished me. They felt they had been betrayed, that the security of the lounges had been breached. It was as though the teachers had been caught with their hands in the cookie jar.

None of them had dared to challenge the administration's position on cola. None of them, on the other hand, seemed to worry about the ethics of ignoring the dictates of the administration. Their only concern seemed to be that they had been caught, and that their Cokes were being taken away!

Not long afterward I got a late-night phone call at our apartment in St. Anthony. Margaretta and I had already gone to bed; it was nearly midnight. I padded out to the kitchen to answer it.

"Why don't you just knock it off, Spencer?" came a male voice I didn't recognize.

"Who is this?"

"Someone with good reason to question your loyalty to the Church. What are you doing at Ricks, anyway?"

By this time I was getting mad. "No wonder you won't identify yourself," I retorted. "People who make anonymous phone calls are cowards!" And I slammed down the receiver.

Back in bed, Margaretta was unruffled. But I was seething, particularly since my loyalty to the Church had been called into question by some zealot who probably wouldn't even think for himself.

That was the first of a series of strange late-night phone calls. One suggested we get out of town. All questioned my commitment as a Mormon. What I had considered a ludicrous situation in need of resolution was apparently hands-off to many people.

By the end of my two years at Ricks, though I remained

totally committed to the Church, I was beginning to have doubts about the practical effectiveness of Mormonism. It wasn't Church doctrine that I struggled with; it was the difficulty translating faith into action.

Bill and I discussed it. He felt the same way, though he was not ready to let his thinking go as far as mine. On the one hand he openly confessed that many of the students were dull and evidently shallow. He did not enjoy the other faculty members and he did not respect the administration. But his loyalty to the Church was complete. He told me one day that even if he came to find that Mormonism was not true, he could never leave the Church.

For myself, I knew that Mormonism was more than a religion. I was coming to see that, as a social system, it touched every part of a member's occupational, social and family life.

I continued to commute twelve miles one way each day from St. Anthony to Rexburg for classes. Each day I passed twice through the little town of Sugar City. One afternoon, on a curve just outside town, I had another experience that focused my growing recognition of the shallowness of the Church.

I stopped to pick up an old man who was hitchhiking. He must have been ninety. Laying his cane in the back seat, he squinted at me through his one good eye (he had a patch over the other one) and thanked me for the lift.

"Been hitchhiking since L.A.," he said. "Spent my Social Security check on a ticket from Anchorage." He winced with pain as he shifted his dilapidated little frame in the front seat.

"Where are you headed?"

He turned his head to focus his good eye on me. "Michigan."

"Michigan! That's a long way, oldtimer."

"I think I have some people there."

"You think? Don't you know?"

"Nope."

"What'll you do if you don't find anybody?"

He eyed me with amusement. "Sonny, do you have any idea how long I've been taking care of myself?"

I laughed.

The old guy was pleasant, polite and good-natured. Obviously no drunk or drifter, he was a sparkling conversationalist.

Since evening was approaching, I invited him to spend the night with Margaretta and me. We fed him supper. But because our apartment was small and Margaretta was not feeling good, we decided to try to find some other place for him to stay the night.

I called my bishop, who finally told me to take him to the local hotel and get him a room and the Church would pay for it. The room cost $5.50.

The next morning I gave him breakfast, packed him a lunch and found him a ride with a gasoline tanker into Montana. I felt good about the experience and was glad to see the Good Samaritan response of the Church. But on Sunday my enthusiasm was dampened.

"Jim," the bishop called as he spotted me coming into church. "Can I talk to you a minute?"

"Sure," I said pleasantly.

In his office, he sat down in a swivel chair behind an old blonde desk, looking apprehensive. "Jim, I need to ask you a question."

"Sure. Fire away."

He looked down at his hands folded protectively in front of him on the desk top. Without looking up he asked, "Was that old man you took to the hotel a member of the Church?"

"No," I said, growing defensive. "He wasn't. Why?"

"Well, I'm afraid we can't pay for the hotel bill. The Church does not authorize us to do this for non-members."

"What kind of position is that?"

He looked up in irritation. "I'm really sorry, Jim, but I don't make the rules. I *obey* them."

I shoved back my chair and stood up. "Bishop, I am not going to tell you what I am thinking." I walked to the door, stopped and turned around. He continued to stare at his hands. I walked out.

I felt angry. What kind of Christianity did not have time for the poor? What was the story of the Good Samaritan all about, anyway? No matter how hard I tried to convince myself otherwise, I realized this was not an isolated incident; it represented Church policy.

One of my last experiences at Ricks was particularly tragic. One morning a baby was found in a ladies' room in one of the girls' dorms. The baby was alive and in good health, but it had been abandoned in a cardboard box.

The identity of the mother was never disclosed. The baby was quietly adopted and, after a minor flap, the decorum of the community remained unmarred.

I was shaken by the implications of the incident. Things like that happened everywhere, of course. But the image of a young girl bearing a child at a religious, middle-class institution and then having to abandon her newborn—or even worse, giving birth alone on the cold tile floor of a restroom—made me sick with pity. Was there no one she could go to? No one who could love and understand her? No parent? No bishop?

I was frustrated by what I saw at Ricks and in my ward and among my friends. The reality of Mormon life did not square with the picture our public relations writers painted of the typical Mormon family: parents and children smiling wholesomely at the world from the pages of paid advertising supplements in *Reader's Digest.*

I was floored when I heard that Utah, the great Mormon state of Deseret, had a higher divorce rate than the national average, and a higher rate of child abuse and teenage suicide.

For the life of me, I could not shake the spectre of the baby in the bathroom. I was having difficulty suppressing the waves of sickening emptiness that I was beginning to feel.

I could not understand a God prejudiced by colored skin. Or a church that could not spare $5.50 for an old gentleman in need, simply because he was not a member. Or family relationships that were orderly but superficial and shallow. Or a school that was isolationist and unable to provide young men and women with basic dialogue on human relationships and problems. I found myself in a no-man's land where obedience was blind and justice monstrous.

I watched helplessly as God's True Church placed tremendous social pressure on young brides to stay constantly pregnant, and then turned a blind eye on the queue of young mothers at the pharmacy for their weekly stash of Valium. I was becoming weary of smiles, stock answers and shallow thinking. I served the Mormon Church with zeal and faithfulness. Indeed, the Church was my god—but now that god was becoming hostile and foreign.

Nevertheless, despite what I saw and heard, I continued to cling to the same hope—that something must be wrong with *me.* Perhaps I was not trying hard enough. That must be the answer. It was, in any case, the only one I could live with: that regardless of my opinions, the Church *had to be right*. It was imperative for me to find a way to bend my will and inferior thinking to line up with the Church. Anything less would cost me my soul. I decided with renewed determination, even desperation, to fit in.

Although I was an honor student, after completing my two years at Ricks I did not apply to graduate. I did not care for a certificate from the school. I had been accepted at Arizona State University and was anxious only to be on my way. I hoped a break from the oppressive, inbred community would clear my head and let me get a renewed perspective on my faith.

8

A FORK IN THE ROAD

Arizona State University in 1971 was everything Ricks College was not. If Ricks had been stodgy and paralyzed, I found ASU decadent and hostile. Walking down the mall, I was confronted with those who had tuned out, shot up or dropped out.

The Students for a Democratic Society, at a booth set up on the mall, publicly advocated radical political change. Gay rights groups and representatives of women's liberation hawked their philosophies in a carnival atmosphere.

Hare Krishnas danced in saffron robes to the jingle of bells tied to their ankles. Advocates of transcendental meditation, Bahaiism, black militarism, chemical religion and every imaginable sect vied for attention on warm desert evenings. Every guru at ASU had his followers.

I was selected as feature editor for the *State Press*, the university newspaper. In that capacity, I came into contact with everyone. Chicanos and blacks sought me out to publicize their causes in the newspaper. I discovered that, rather than being the radical editorialist who terrorized

Ricks College, I was a conservative homebody out of sync with what was happening in the real world.

In addition to being a full-time student, I was working forty hours a week writing radio copy for Associated Press.   But pressure from three years of hectically juggling my roles as full-time student, husband, father and journalist was taking its toll. After one year at ASU, and another session of summer school, I began to suffer tremendous bouts of fatigue and experience increased family and financial pressure.

One afternoon during summer session, I walked out of the journalism building and was nearly knocked over by the roasting 110-degree heat. When I arrived home, I found Margaretta sitting directly under the "swamp cooler" air-conditioner in the hallway of our mobile home. Sweat was pouring off her and her hair was hanging limp. She simply could not take the climatic change from the cold winters and cool summers of Idaho.

"Man, you look awful," I said.

"Thanks a lot."

"No kidding, honey, are you O.K.?"

Her chin began to tremble. I sat down beside her and put my arm around her. "What's the matter?"

She began to cry. "Everything's the matter! You're never home. You're either working or in school. I'm left here all day long with a four-year-old and the heat is unbearable and we don't have enough money and—"

"Hey, wait! I know things aren't easy. But I don't know what to do about it. I'm doing the best I can."

"I want to go home!"

"You mean to Idaho?"

"Yes. I want to take Erin and live with my folks for the rest of the summer."

"What about me?"

"You stay here and go to school. That's all you really care about anyhow!"

"Hey, give me a break!"

"I'm sorry. It's not your fault, I know. But I just can't take any more of this. I need to get away."

I knew Margaretta was right. I couldn't stand the thought of my family's leaving me, even for the summer, but I didn't know what else to do. So I put her and Erin on the bus.

I continued to go to school the rest of the first summer session. But it was so hard without my wife and daughter that, on one weekend between sessions, I drove eighteen hours nonstop to visit them in Idaho for a few days. While I was there, I talked to the manager of the weekly newspaper in Rexburg, who offered me a job. I accepted.

We returned to Arizona just long enough to sell our mobile home. We settled into our second small apartment in St. Anthony, and Margaretta went back to work at the bank.

In 1972 the nation was healing from the wounds of Vietnam and Richard Nixon was about to landslide into his second term. As we settled in to our new jobs, we began to find for the first time a kind of normalcy in our married life. For once I was working a regular schedule and at last we had enough money. Things seemed to be looking up. Soon we bought a home. I taught Erin to ride her bike. I played chess one night each week. And both Margaretta and I became active in the Church.

Although our circumstances had stabilized, however, inwardly I was not satisfied. A nagging sense of emptiness haunted the nooks and crannies of my mind. Something within me, in quiet moments, cried out that my life was shallow and unfulfilling. What could be wrong? What was missing?

For one thing, I was beginning to feel genuine disappointment in the Church. I was becoming convinced that something basic was missing. I had tried, God knew, to fit into the organization. In fact, I *had* fit in—so successfully that no one knew I was dissatisfied.

But I was beginning to see that, despite Mormonism's articulated focus on family and community, no one was really getting close to anyone else. They didn't want anyone to know what they were really like. They didn't want anyone to know that they were not perfect, that they had problems. Margaretta and I had lots of friends, but no close friends. Though I longed to share with others on an intimate level, my relationships with others in our ward remained superficial. No one seemed to feel free to discuss personal fears or failures.

Margaretta and I led a Young Marrieds group that met once a month for a gospel lesson and evening of socializing. One night I polled the group to see what level of communication was taking place in their marriages. I passed out slips of paper asking for anonymous responses to questions like, "Have you ever discussed divorce?" and, "How often do you have a serious argument?" According to this informal poll, absolutely no marriage problems existed in our group. But, in fact, I knew our ward experienced its share of marriage breakups. And I read that, corroborating what I had heard at Ricks, Mormons experience a rate of divorce higher than the national average.

Still, we continued the charade. All was well in Zion. And on Sunday mornings we all smiled at one another across the rows.

Once released from the grind of college life, I found I had time to investigate my own inner development. I had come a long way from my Navy days, and even from the excitement of my new involvement in the Church and with my "father" in the faith, Ed Ingles. A year or so after our marriage, Margaretta and I had moved from Santa Ana and lost touch with Ed and Martha. And my desire to believe what he told me about Church doctrine, my need to be accepted—all this seemed like a long time ago.

I knew it was time to search for roots. I continued looking within myself and at the roots of Mormonism to see if I could discover something to explain the emptiness I felt.

The summer of 1972 Margaretta and I decided to include in our vacation some of the historic sites of Mormonism. We traveled to Illinois and Missouri where much early Mormon history had been enacted.

We visited Nauvoo, Illinois, the community on the banks of the Mississippi River that Joseph Smith had, by 1844, built into the largest, most thriving city in the state. Joseph had been mayor of Nauvoo as well as commanding general of the militia. He built a beautiful mansion called Nauvoo House.

We visited the grave sites of Joseph and his brother Hyrum, who had been murdered by an angry mob while being held in jail in nearby Carthage, Illinois. We visited that jail, and the guide showed us what he said were Hyrum's bloodstains on the wooden floor of the cell.

One hot July afternoon we pulled our little travel trailer into Independence, Missouri. Latter-day Saints are convinced that Jackson County, Missouri, is the actual site of the Garden of Eden, and that Independence carries strategic importance in God's plan for the Second Coming of Christ.

Margaretta, Erin and I walked through a large, green, vacant field near downtown Independence, selected by Joseph Smith as the site for a large temple. This temple was to mark the point to which Jesus Christ would return at His second advent. Joseph had even laid a cornerstone for that temple. Faithful Mormons expect that the eventual construction of this temple will signal the imminent return of Christ.

At an adjacent intersection, on three corners, stood buildings representing three different Mormon organizations, each claiming to be the one True Church.

Across the street stood my own Church's modern visitors' center, the most beautiful and impressive of the structures.

Alongside stood the World Headquarters for the Reorganized Church of Jesus Christ of Latter-day Saints—the denomination behind the frame structure I had seen in Tustin, California, just after my conversion. The Reorganites have about 250,000 members and claim to be the legal continuation of the church Joseph Smith established.

The Reorganites say that Joseph, in the presence of many witnesses, and upon numerous occasions, designated his son, Joseph Smith III, to succeed him as prophet, seer and revelator of the Mormon Church. Court actions in Ohio in 1880 and in Missouri in 1894 had upheld their legal claim to succession.

Across the street from the Reorganized World Headquarters, and at the end of the vacant field, stood a small, unassuming building—the visitors' center of the Church of Christ (Temple Lot). An elderly man inside told Margaretta and me that they had fewer than 3,000 members meeting in about thirty congregations, led by twelve apostles. The most interesting thing about this organization, we learned, is that they own the property upon which the great temple is to be built.

All three groups with holdings in Independence recognize that the temple must be built on the spot dedicated by Joseph Smith. So a stalemate exists: Jesus cannot return until the temple is built; the Church of Christ (Temple Lot) is in no position financially to build the temple; and the two organizations that could build it cannot because they don't have access to the property. Since all three groups claim each of the other groups is apostate, there is little hope they will work out an agreement.

History came alive for me on our trip through the Midwest. I was projected back in time to when the saints walked the streets of "Beautiful City" (the meaning of the word *Nauvoo*). I could almost see the prophet Joseph, shoulder-to-shoulder with the saints, as they carved out pioneer history.

But the trip posed a new and interesting question: Where did all these other Mormons fit in? They, like the Utah Church, read and accepted the Book of Mormon. They, too, believed that God had restored His Church through the prophet Joseph Smith. And they, too, believed in the restored priesthood—the power to act for God. So where had they gone wrong? Why were they considered apostate?

I had been taught that, after Joseph Smith was killed, the Church had gathered in Nauvoo for a great conference and that "the mantle of the Prophet fell upon Brigham Young." Utah Church historians said that Brigham's face had taken on the appearance of Joseph and that he had begun to speak in Joseph's voice as he addressed the people. Apparently there had been no doubt about how God wanted to continue the Church. All the faithful followed Brigham Young to Utah.

But now I was presented with evidence to the contrary. Many, if not most, of the faithful Mormons did *not* follow Brigham Young to Utah.

The Crow Creek group, which became the Church of Christ (Temple Lot), did not follow Brigham. Neither did the New Organization, another splinter group. Or the

Strangites. Many groups, I learned, contend that true Mormonism never did get to Utah.

One of the early giants of Mormonism, for example, and one of those closest to Joseph Smith (who probably had the most influence on him), was Sidney Rigdon, a former Campbellite preacher. Rigdon contested Brigham Young for leadership of the Church. He led a contingent of the Church to Greencastle, Pennsylvania. Rigdon denounced Brigham Young's teaching on the plurality of gods, plural marriage and baptism for the dead. An outgrowth of that Mormon group today is the Bickertonites, which numbers fifty congregations.

The Strangite organization, founded by James J. Strang, claims to be "the one and original Church of Jesus Christ of Latter-day Saints." Strang was the only successor to Church leadership with written credentials from Joseph Smith. Strang continued Joseph's penchant for translation of ancient writings, translating *The Plates of Laban* and *The Voree Record*, a record ostensibly found under an oak tree near Voree, Wisconsin.

Gradually it began to dawn on me that all four parts of a typical Mormon testimony could be recited by any one of these groups. All believed Joseph Smith was a prophet, that the Book of Mormon was the Word of God, that they belonged to the Restored Church, and that a prophet was the head of the Church today.

So in reality, there was one main question up for discussion: Who was that prophet today? And, working backwards: Who had been the rightful successor to Joseph Smith? I was beginning to see that my Utah Church could not base its claim to authenticity solely on either Joseph Smith *or* the Book of Mormon. They were obliged to prove that theirs actually was the Church Joseph had founded, and that Brigham Young was Joseph Smith's rightful successor.

In my heart I was certain that all these other prophets were false. A seed of doubt had sprouted during my trip to Nauvoo, however, and before we returned home, I dropped a card into the box at the visitors' center of the Reorganized Church, asking for more information.

Events were shaping for confrontations that would have serious and long-lasting effects on me and my family.

9

A CRACK IN THE FOUNDATION

Back home after our Nauvoo trip, I settled in at the newspaper while Margaretta returned to the bank. Outwardly things continued to go well for us, but behind the closed doors of our new home an uneasiness was settling in. We seemed to be caught in a rut. Though we were fully active in our ward, neither of us felt a sense of direction for our lives.

Margaretta would not discuss my waning confidence in the Church. But she did acknowledge the general restlessness we both were feeling.

"What is *wrong* with me?" she asked one evening after dinner.

"What do you mean?" I responded, although I knew what she was going to say.

"We just seem to live from day to day. We go to work. We come home. By the time we get Erin in bed it's time to go to sleep, just to start over tomorrow. Isn't there more to life than just making it from day to day, from paycheck to paycheck?"

"But everybody seems to have that problem."

"Jim, we aren't everybody. We're *us!* Where is our direction? You're the one who used to say people have a right to be excited about life. What are you excited about?"

"Not much."

"That's what I mean. Neither am I. What's wrong with us?"

"I don't know," I replied thoughtfully. "But I sure know what you're talking about. And you know, I'm having some problems figuring out where the Church fits in with all this."

"Jim, our problems are not the Church."

"Are you sure?"

"Maybe the Church isn't perfect. But we have to take responsibility for our own lives. If I'm not happy, it's not the fault of the Church. It's my own fault."

"O.K., but the Church is supposed to be perfect."

"I think it is."

"Let me finish. The Church is supposed to be perfect. We have a living prophet who is in touch with God. We go to meetings led by men who are called by inspiration to guide us. But Margaretta, those meetings are *boring* and you know it!"

"I'm not going to talk about the Church."

"O.K., but answer me this. Why don't we feel life in those meetings? Why aren't we getting anything out of church? I get up on Sunday, spend nearly all day in church and I feel worse at the end of the day than I did at the beginning."

"I don't know why these discussions always have to come back to the Church."

"Because something is wrong!"

"If something is wrong," she said firmly, "it's *us.*"

"You know, honey, I have always thought that. You know I've always said, 'The Church is perfect, but the people are imperfect.' But I'm not so sure anymore that the Church is perfect. Oh, I know it was set up to *be* perfect, but the Church Christ established in the first century was perfect and it fell. That's why God had to restore it through Joseph Smith. How do I know the same thing hasn't happened again, now?"

"I don't care. I think we can solve our own problems. There is something wrong with our marriage. Something wrong with us. We just aren't interested in anything."

"Yeah, I know."

"And even if there *were* something wrong with the Church, I wouldn't want to know it. I was raised in the Church and I'll die in it. Nothing is going to change that. And frankly, Jim, your attitude doesn't make me very happy. I want you to remember one thing: I married you in the temple. That's very important to me. I don't like some of the things I hear you saying. You can blame our problems on the Church if you want to, but that isn't going to solve anything."

I was silent. She got up, started for the living room, then stopped. "Let me say this plainly. If you ever leave the Church, it will be the end of our marriage." She continued to look at me for a moment, then turned and left the kitchen.

I knew she meant what she said. And because St. Anthony was her hometown, because her parents still lived there, because she knew almost everyone in town, she was not even willing to consider the possibility of major problems in the Church.

Given Margaretta's adamant stand, I was dismayed to find two middle-aged men at our door one evening who introduced themselves as missionaries of the Reorganized Church of Jesus Christ of Latter-day Saints. Margaretta shot me an irritated look as I invited them in.

They were dressed neatly but casually. One of them, Elder Zellinger, was a handsome man of about 45, perhaps six feet tall, with wavy black hair. As I ushered them into the living room, he explained that he had been a full-time missionary for fifteen years. To him, I knew, full-time meant lifetime. Elder Batenhorst looked to be about 60, paunchy and more relaxed than his colleague. He said he was the principal of a school in Idaho Falls.

Once seated on the couch, Elder Zellinger looked directly at me. "We have the card you filled out at the World Headquarters in Independence last summer, Mr. Spencer," he said politely. "That's why we're here. What can we do for you?"

I was a little taken aback. I had expected him to launch into a prepared discussion in order to reason me out of the Utah Church and into the Reorganized Church.

"Well," I began, "I don't really know what I want. I'm just having some problems with things as they are in the Church and I don't know what to do about it."

"I can understand that," Elder Zellinger said. "What in particular are you having problems with?"

"Well, for instance, I have a problem with the fact that my Church will not ordain blacks into the priesthood. How do you feel about that?"

"We ordain blacks. God is no respecter of persons."

"I'd be very interested in pursuing that subject with you, but let me ask you a couple other questions. What about polygamy and plurality of gods?"

"We are neither polygamous nor polytheistic."

"How can you not be, in light of the fact that Joseph Smith was both?"

"Well, you see, that's where we disagree with the Utah Church. We do not believe Joseph Smith was either polygamous or polytheistic."

"You *don't?*"

"No, we don't."

"How do you get to that position? In the King Follett Discourse, Joseph Smith makes it patently clear that he taught plurality of gods."

"It is our position," he said, "that the King Follett Discourse was not recorded accurately. What you need to remember, Mr. Spencer, is that Brigham Young had a vested interest, since he was a polygamist, in tying Joseph Smith to that practice. The same is true with the plurality of gods idea. In fact, most of the doctrines that are 'way out' in the Utah Church can be traced directly to Brigham Young—the Adam-God Theory, Blood Atonement, and so on."

I spent three hours talking to the two missionaries. They gave me much information comparing the practices and doctrines of the Utah Church with the Reorganized Church.

At the end of our time together, I thanked them for sharing with me. And that night I made one important commitment to myself—that, despite what Margaretta had said, I would look even deeper into the whole history of Mormonism. I could see there were many different opinions about what had happened in the early days of the Church. And I knew that before I could make any real judgments about the validity of any of the claims of the various factions, I was going to have to dig.

I knew a little Church history. I knew, as a good Mormon, that shortly after Joseph Smith began the Church in 1830 in New York, he moved to Ohio, then Missouri and eventually Illinois, where he was killed. I knew that Brigham Young had led a large contingent of the Illinois population in flight from Nauvoo across the frozen Mississippi to winter quarters in Iowa. On July 24, 1847, Young and his followers had entered the Salt Lake Valley, where he is supposed to have uttered his famous line, "This is the place."

Brigham, according to all accounts, ruled the new state of Deseret with an iron hand. He was a genius at organization and colonization. Under his skillful leadership, innovative irrigation plans were executed that made the desert "blossom as a rose" from St. George in southern Utah (referred to affectionately as "Dixie") to the reaches of southeastern Idaho and northwestern Wyoming.

Brigham Young was not only the religious leader, but the political governor of "Zion." The United States government watched the territory of Utah warily as Brigham governed it. The Mormons, with their strange religious views, temple ceremonies, polygamy, plurality of gods and iron-fisted authoritarian priesthood, were considered candidates for rebellion.

Many Washington congressmen still remembered the Mormons as the followers of the strange "prophet" from Illinois who had initiated an independent campaign for the United States Presidency. The country was gearing up for the Civil War, which erupted just thirteen years after the Mormons entered Utah, and Washington was in no mood for a confrontation in the West. In addition, there was already trouble on the Mexican border and with the Indian wars. Washington needed, at least temporarily, the friendship of Brigham Young.

And so the debate over the official government position on Utah was tabled, although the discussion about Mormon polygamy—considered outrageous by the nation as a whole—continued to be a topic in both houses of Congress.

As I mentally set my sails to investigate the roots of the Mormon Church, I determined to go to the original sources. I was not going to be satisfied with secondhand information.

Then I realized I had been unwittingly prepared for this investigation from the earliest days of my association with Mormonism. One of the first purchases I had made as a new believer was a series of books called *The Journal of Discourses*. The 26-volume set had been on sale in a Deseret bookstore, specially priced at that time at $50.00.

The Journal of Discourses was a compilation of most of the important sermons of the Church from Brigham Young's earliest days. I had seldom used the books; they had just gathered dust in my library. But I knew that much of the key to the history of the Church would be found in the sermons of the early leadership.

As I pulled one of the black volumes from my shelf, I suspected that, whatever the outcome of my research, there would be no turning back.

10

WHERE ARE YOU, JESUS?

Margaretta and I took our seats in the auditorium. We had just finished attending the 100-member gospel doctrine class I taught. Now we were assembling for Fast and Testimony Meeting, which took place the first Sunday of every month immediately after Sunday school. On each side of the auditorium, a young man stood with microphone in hand to accommodate those ward members who wanted to "bear their testimonies."

The bishop opened the meeting by calling on one of his counselors to testify. Then one after another of the faithful stood to their feet and testified: "Jesus is the Christ, this is God's true Church, Joseph Smith was a prophet and the Church is led by a living prophet today." Other testimonies would relate how the Church or the bishop or one's husband or wife had done something loving and wonderful that confirmed the fact that Mormonism was the only true Church and that we were indeed fortunate to be Mormons.

Fast and Testimony Meeting had always been a mixed blessing for me. On the one hand, the meetings tended to be boring. We usually had several older saints dominate the meetings by refusing to relinquish the microphone while they related a travelogue covering the last thirty years of their Church activity. On the other hand, Fast and Testimony Meeting had provided some of the most spiritual moments of my life. Sometimes someone would say something that would stir my soul in a marvelous way.

This particular Sunday in November 1973 was one of those special times. In fact, it would mark a turning point in my life, though I would not recognize it as such for some time.

To commence the testimonies, an elderly farmer in an ill-fitting, wide-lapeled suit rose to his feet a few rows in front of us. He began to tell how much his affiliation with the Church meant. During the fall harvest, he said, while he had been working sixteen hours a day getting in the wheat, his faithful wife had driven out to the combine every night with a hot meal for him. He thanked God he belonged to a Church that taught its people the meaning of proper family relationships.

On my right a young mother stood up wearing a long print dress revealing that she was in the early months of pregnancy. She had a blonde child less than a year old in her arms and her husband wrestled two more at her side. She said how much she appreciated the primary program at church. How thrilled she was for the privilege of working with the little ones every Tuesday afternoon! How much they taught her about her heavenly Father!

I looked around the auditorium at nearly 300 people. Most were under 45 and most had several young children, though here and there I spotted a gray head. I knew that all these people were absolutely sincere in what they said and believed. They were genuinely happy to be part of an organization which, in a world of uncertainty and violence,

promoted the virtues of decency, honesty and family to-
getherness.

The problem was, I could no longer take at face value the
vague, emotive statements made by True Believers. So long
as my fretting had been only internal—so long as I only *felt*
there was something wrong in Zion—I was not free to
challenge the picture of the Church systematically provided
us from Salt Lake. But since I had made the agonizing
decision to unwrap my mind and look at the Church objectively, I was discovering with sinking heart that there were
serious, foundation-level problems in Mormonism.

I had intensified my investigation of Church history six
months earlier, right after the Reorganite missionaries had
visited our home. During this time I had patiently searched
the *Journal of Discourses,* as well as *The Documented History of
the Church.* In a way I wished I hadn't even begun my
investigation, since I feared where it was leading me.

For one thing, it was forcing me to take a hard look at my
whole spiritual foundation. I cannot describe the sense of
weariness and loss that began to haunt me. The Mormon
Church was my whole life. The thought of giving it up was
unbearable.

And I was beginning to realize that if I continued my
research, I might come to a point of theological incom-
patibility and be left with nothing at all.

In my investigation, I had chosen to look not only at the
roots of Mormonism, but also at the fruits. And as I did, I
could no longer swallow (in testimonies like the ones I was
now hearing) the recounting of its virtues.

Although we prided ourselves in our religious devotion
to our families, for example, I had personally witnessed the
alienation and emptiness in Mormon family life. I had seen
the backward character of the students at Ricks College. For
ten years I had tasted the banality and shallow provin-

cialism of the Mormon Church-state. And now, as I opened my eyes and looked objectively at the facts, I was forced to admit that "Happy Valley in the Rockies" was not happy at all. As I listened to men and women sing the praises of Mormonism, I knew the reality behind it: The Church failed to produce lasting marriages and healthy homes.

Statistics told me that Utah, the great Mormon state of Deseret, had a consistently higher divorce rate than the nation as a whole.[1] It consistently led the national average in the rate of teenage suicide.[2] And, within the citadel of Mormonism, child abuse was rampant.[3]

I was later to learn of Utah's inflated rate of larceny,[4] corporate crime,[5] and sharply rising rate of suicide among women.[6] Also in Utah, twenty percent of all homicide victims were children under the age of fifteen—a rate five times the national average.[7]

My study, only six months old at the time of the Fast and Testimony Meeting, was bringing me to the brink of despair. As blackness began to enfold my world, I longed for a glimmer of hope.

Now, as yet another stood to testify that Sunday morning in November, hope was about to dawn. The man who rose to speak was a friend—not close, but someone I talked to from time to time. He was a schoolteacher, outwardly pa-

---

[1] *Deseret News*, February 11, 1976.

[2] *Deseret News*, September 3, 1979.

[3] *Salt Lake Tribune*, June 26 and August 13, 1982.

[4] *Uniform Crime Reports*, Federal Bureau of Investigation, 1980, or World Almanac, 1983, pp. 966-967.

[5] *Salt Lake Tribune*, August 25, 1982.

[6] *Deseret News*, September 21, 1979.

[7] *Salt Lake Tribune*, June 26 and August 13, 1982.

tient and loving with his students as well as with his own children. I knew that he had serious problems at home. He had confided, much to my surprise, that he and his wife nearly had divorced at the beginning of the school year.

His testimony was not unusual. In fact, what he said did not differ much from what any of the others had said. He began with the customary "My friends, I know that Jesus is the Christ. . . ."

And when he said that, the same thing happened to me that happened regularly in testimony meetings. Whenever anyone said, "I know that Jesus is the Christ," the hair stood up on my arms and on the back of my neck. Sometimes I even began to weep. I could not cry when I heard about a great tragedy, or even when someone died. But I often cried at certain statements about Jesus Christ.

This was a little embarrassing. I had a reputation for being softhearted in testimony meetings, though I never cried at stories about the Church's family programs, or the Scouting program, or when someone mentioned Joseph Smith. My crying was reserved for expressions of devotion for Jesus. I had come to believe that these displays of emotion were a manifestation of the Holy Spirit.

But this time something else happened, too. As I began to weep at my friend's statement, something clicked in my mind. Perhaps there was something salvageable in my religious life, I thought. Perhaps there was a bottom-line Something that was real in my experience. Perhaps, in fact, that *Something* might be *Someone.*

As all the points of faith in the Church had begun to crumble away during the past few months, a form was emerging out of the wreckage with increasing clarity. That form was the Person of Jesus.

I had nowhere else to turn. I knew all too well the costs involved in a search such as mine. Were I to leave the

Church, I would be a social outcast in a community in which nearly everyone was a Church member. My scorn would be doubled because I was not only a member of the Mormon community, but a respected leader.

My wife's parents would never understand if I were compelled to leave. Neither would my friends. Even my job on the newspaper, in a community 90 percent Mormon, could be threatened.

Worst of all, I knew what Margaretta's reaction would be. There was no doubt in my mind that she was not prepared for this kind of social upheaval. She would never leave the Church and would deeply resent my doing so. I knew in the depths of my heart that if I left the Church, *Margaretta would leave me.*

In this dark moment, all my religious moorings were torn loose. It was a time to return to basics. I had to ask myself what, if anything, I *could* believe. When I reduced everything to essential, believable minimums, was anything salvageable for me in Mormonism? Was anything left as an unchallenged point of faith? And what about this Man who, when acknowledged as the Christ, brought tears to my eyes?

That morning in Fast and Testimony meeting marked the beginning of a recurring experience I began to call my "tapestry" experience. As I continued my search, whether reading or in a meeting or simply meditating on my spiritual condition, it seemed that I was continually drawn back to think about my relationship with Jesus Christ. He seemed to represent the focus of everything that bore any real importance. He faded in and out of my awareness, ever present yet somehow elusive.

As a Mormon, of course, I recognized Him as the Savior. The name *Jesus Christ* was part of the name of my Church, written on the exterior of every Mormon building. We closed each prayer "in the name of Thy beloved Son, Amen." But I was beginning to get the impression that, though I talked a lot about Jesus, He was theoretical. I got the impression that He was supposed to be more real. Maybe, more correctly, I began to hope that He could be more real *to me*.

One thing was certain. I realized that if I were to make any sense out of my religious life, I would have to make contact with Jesus Christ.

11

THE SUGAR CITY CURVE

The Presbyterian minister leaned on his snow shovel on the steps of his church and grinned at me as I drove slowly by. On an impulse, I parked my pickup in the middle of the street and walked over to talk to him. He was average height, slender, with dark brown hair. He must have been forty, but he looked no more than 25. Except for the black shirt and clerical collar, he bore a striking resemblance to Roy Rogers. I was surprised there was no one in his congregation to shovel the walks.

"Hi!" I said. "Looks like you're overqualified for this job."

He smiled. "I don't know about that, but I enjoy the exercise." He stuck out his hand. "I'm Pastor Shaw."

"Jim Spencer. Nice to meet you. Got a minute?"

"Sure. What's on your mind?"

"I'll come right to the point. I'm a Mormon elder, but I'm looking for information about Jesus Christ. Do you know anything about Him?"

Pastor Shaw eyed me intently, sizing me up. Was I putting him on? Apparently deciding I was serious, he smiled broadly and said, "Call me Mike. Come on into my office."

His office was in the basement of the church, located just blocks from my house. The walls were lined with books and an old wooden desk was stacked high with papers. The pastor flopped into a wooden swivel chair and motioned me into a padded folding chair. "Now, start from the beginning. How can I serve you?"

"Well, Pastor, as I said, I'm a Mormon elder, and I don't expect to change. But I have a problem. In fact, I have several problems—with the Church. I guess I need to say that I believe the Book of Mormon is true and that I believe Joseph Smith was the prophet of the Restoration. But I'm afraid I'm beginning to doubt that the Church today is in touch with God."

Mike looked understanding, so I continued, "I don't know why I'm talking to you about this. After all, if I really believe that God's Church fell away in the first century, that means your Presbyterian Church has nothing to say to me."

"That's true," Mike said gently.

"Look," I said. "I'm confused. I don't really want to talk about churches. I think I need to talk about God. Somehow I think—I hope—you can tell me something about Him."

"Jim, I don't want to talk about churches, either. But I want to ask you a question. May I?"

"You might as well. I can't think of a good question myself!"

"You're looking for God, right?"

"I sure am."

"And you have already identified your source of information about God as Jesus?"

"Yes. I think Jesus is the only One who could speak really authoritatively about God."

"Then it's simple," Mike said.

"It is?"

"Sure. You want information about God? You think Jesus has the answer? Then ask *Him*."

"You mean prayer?"

""More or less."

"But I do pray."

"Jim, I'm not talking about some kind of formal prayer. I'm talking about having a conversation with God—with Jesus."

I sat in silence. I had read everything—the Bible and the Book of Mormon. I had talked to people. And I had prayed for guidance, asking God to lead me to the truth. But I suspected Mike was talking about something radically different. If my life up till now had been an incomplete jigsaw puzzle, this might be the first of the missing pieces.

He continued, "What you are looking for is not religion. You're looking for a relationship."

I left Mike's office deep in thought. I had made a commitment to talk to him further. And now, as I walked back to the truck, I wondered if I could figure out how to talk to Jesus.

A few days later, a second puzzle piece fell into place.

My family and I were visiting my hometown in Wyoming. While there, I learned that my old childhood friend, Fred Johnson, had recently moved back to Basin. Fred was the third member of the gang that included my friend Lee and myself. I had not talked to Fred for several years, ever since Lee and I had heard he had gotten religion at a Billy Graham crusade in Kansas City.

Fred had attended the Conservative Baptist church in Basin when we were kids. His father was an active layman in that church. I had even attended with Fred sometimes. Later, in high school, we had drunk a lot together and I knew he wasn't too religious. But maybe since his experience in Kansas City, he would have something to say to me.

As I pulled into his driveway, Fred walked out the back door of his house. Seeing me was apparently a shock. "Is that Jimmie Spencer in that car?"

I jumped out. "Freddy Johnson, you haven't changed a bit!" Throwing my arm over his shoulder, I walked with him into the house.

"Cynthia, look at this!"

Inside, I greeted Fred's wife, who had lived just a few doors from me when I was in high school. After a half-hour of reminiscing, Fred asked how things were going in my life. He knew I was a Mormon. In fact, I had spoken about it at length with his father in Basin while Margaretta and I were on our honeymoon. Stan had expressed genuine concern and disappointment in my Mormonism.

"Well, buddy," I said, "I'm having some problems. I am beginning to doubt that the Mormon Church is where I belong."

"Well, Jim, I'm sure if you take your time, you'll find what is right."

Glad for his tact and patience, I asked, "What *is* right, Fred?"

He smiled, leaned back on the couch and put his hands behind his head. I was surprised to see how athletic he still was. "Well, Jim"—he chose his words carefully—"I guess the important thing is not where you go to church, but what your relationship is with Jesus Christ."

Bingo! My pulse quickened. "What do you mean?"

"I mean, I'm not talking about religion at all. Let me ask you this. What *is* a Christian?"

"That's what I'm trying to find out."

"Well, I think a Christian is someone who is a disciple of Jesus Christ."

"I've never thought of it exactly like that."

"Well, the idea is that if Jesus is God, then we need to worship and serve Him. If you do that, you're a Christian."

"Well, I know He's the Savior."

"Is He *your* Savior?"

"How do you mean?"

"Well, I don't think He can be your Savior theoretically. I think that's a personal thing. Once again, if He's God, and you worship Him and Him alone, I guess then He would be your *personal* Savior."

"You know, Fred, you sure are eloquent for an old country boy."

He smiled, got up from the couch and looked out the window. "Jimbo, the question is simply this: 'What think ye of Christ? Whose son is he?'" He turned quickly. "Hey! I think you're going to do just fine. Can I tell you what God requires of you?"

"Please."

"That you seek Him with your whole heart."

"I think I've begun that process."

"Then let me promise you one thing. 'Everyone who asks receives, and he who seeks finds, and to him who knocks it will be opened.'"

"More and more eloquent. No kidding, Fred. I need to find something!"

"Relax. Take your time. It's going to be fine."

As I left Fred's that afternoon, somehow I felt that the emptiness in my life was beginning to take a definite shape.

A few weeks later, a third puzzle piece dropped into place—a strange experience that solved no problems, but showed me the bankruptcy of most sources in spiritual truth.

I had traveled to Butte, Montana, on business. While

away from home, I saw more clearly than ever that, despite all my religious pretensions, I was a spiritual failure. My marriage was less than successful; Margaretta and I were continuing to experience futility and even a growing awareness of drifting apart. My work at the newspaper was beginning to be a real trial. I was looking for answers and failing to find them. I even considered giving up my search altogether. I was hitting bottom, incapable of getting my life together.

One morning in Butte I was having breakfast in a cafe, weak with weariness at having to face a new day. If only I could talk with someone who might be able to tell me something more about God.

Then a man walked into the cafe wearing black pants, a black shirt and a large crucifix.

Maybe God has directed this Catholic priest to this cafe, I thought, *so that I can talk to him.*

I approached him, introduced myself and said, "Father, can I talk with you a minute?"

He looked at me blankly, then smiled. "Hey, man, I'm no priest. I just wear black clothes."

"But the crucifix," I stammered, embarrassed.

"Oh, yeah, I'm into religion. But I'm no Catholic."

"Are you *any* kind of Christian?"

"Christian? No, I don't think so. Not formally."

"What are you?"

"I'm a free spirit, man. I worship the great god Manitoba. I smoke a little dope. I really like sex. I travel a lot. I have a wife and a couple of kids somewhere in Minnesota. Want a joint?"

The whole scene was ludicrous. If I hadn't been so drained emotionally I would have been angry. There I was, discouraged, hopeless. And when I attempted to turn to God, I met someone crazier than myself!

I drove home alternately chuckling and shaking my head in disbelief. Obviously there were no answers. God was not alive. Everything was a great cosmic joke.

It was in January 1974, when I felt I had exhausted every avenue of approach to God, that He acted, quickly and simply.

After my return to Idaho, I was commuting to work one morning from St. Anthony to Rexburg. I drove through the little village of Sugar City, where I had picked up the old man hitchhiker several years before. I was negotiating a turn out of Sugar City that I called the Sugar City Curve— an S-shaped curve made up of two ninety-degree turns, a hard right followed by a hard left. It takes about sixty seconds to make the transit. On the Sugar City Curve, the miracle took place.

I entered the curve a self-centered intellectual failure who, after ten years on a treadmill of religious performance, was about as far from knowing God as I had been when I joined the Mormon Church. I was sick of myself. Sick of religion. Sick of life.

Since several people had told me that there was such a thing as personal contact with God, or Jesus, or whoever, I longed to make that contact. I thought it must, as Mike Shaw had suggested, come through prayer. So as I drove, I prayed.

"God," I said, "where are You? Where am I going? What am I supposed to do?"

These were simple, direct, heartfelt questions, to which I did not actually expect an answer. To my amazement, I received one, not in an audible voice, but one that was nonetheless real. As a rational person, I knew it was a rational experience. I sensed I was actually communicating with God.

Well, Jim, came the response, *let's start at the beginning. The problem is, you are doing things your own way. You say you want to find Me. O.K., here's how to do it. Turn your life over to Me.*

I must be crazy! I thought. *I'm having a two-way conversation in my head.*

But Mike had said I needed to talk to God. Fred said I needed a personal experience with Christ. Maybe this was it. Just in case it was, I wasn't about to pass up the chance.

"O.K., God," I said. "You say I'm supposed to *what?*"

Give Me your life.

"Yeah, right. But what do You mean?"

You don't seem to be listening.

"I am listening. I'm just not understanding. Do You mean do what those radio evangelists tell you—'give your heart to Jesus'?"

That's it.

"But I don't even know what that means."

It means that you give Me permission to do anything with you that I want.

"What do you mean by *anything?*"

Anything means anything.

"You mean like going to Africa and spending the rest of my life converting the natives?"

Exactly.

"You're kidding."

Try Me.

"What do I get out of it?"

Now you're kidding.

"What do You mean?"

Son, you have made a complete wreck of your life. You don't know your right hand from your left. I am offering to take over your life and run it for you. That may or may not include Africa. But let Me tell you this: I love you more than you can possibly understand, and I am very trustworthy.

Suddenly something snapped within me. Without understanding it, somehow I gave in. I gave up. I believed God was asking me to give Him my life, as if it had some value. I believed God was accepting me. I believed in His power to heal my life. I believed in *Him*.

"That's it," I said aloud. "*I believe*. O.K., Lord, I give You my life, for what it's worth. If You can use it, go ahead. I trust You and I'm sick of myself. Please do whatever You will. Only don't leave me!"

I won't.

I had no idea of the full implications of the talk I had with God that day. It would take weeks for me to recognize the deep significance of those sixty seconds when I said yes to Him on the Sugar City Curve.

That afternoon I felt an irresistible desire to read the Bible. So after supper I found a copy of a New Testament called *Good News for Modern Man* (I had no idea where I got it) and went down to the basement by myself. What I read put the finishing touches on the contact begun earlier that day.

The Testament fell open to the first chapter of the book of Romans. I don't know how many times previously I had read Romans, but tonight something seemed to be different. Something was *new*. My eyes fell upon verses 16 and 17:

> I have complete confidence in the gospel; it is God's power to save all who believe. . . . For the gospel reveals how God puts people right with himself: it is through faith from beginning to end.

What I read puzzled me because, on the surface, it seemed to contradict clearly stated Mormon doctrine. I grabbed my King James Version missionary Bible to make sure the translations agreed. They did.

The passage in Romans talked about getting right with God; that was exactly what I was interested in. I had tried for ten years to get right with God. Tried to please Him through obedience to the law of tithing, the Word of Wisdom, perfect attendance at meetings, faithfulness in my duties. But the problem was, down deep in my heart, I was no more right with God than when I started.

Laying the Book aside for a moment, I remembered a conversation I had had a few weeks earlier with an old patriarch in the Church. President Allen had been a member for more than seventy years. He was a small man, just over five feet, but carried himself proudly and seemed to have things under control in his life. He had been a stake president for twenty years, serving with tireless energy. I had stopped him in the hallway before sacrament meeting.

"President, can I ask you a question?"

"Sure, son, of course."

"Are you certain you are going to the Celestial Kingdom when you die?"

The question hit him hard. "Why do you ask?"

"I'm not sure. I just feel I'm on a treadmill. I don't seem to be getting anywhere in my spiritual life."

"Well, we all have dry seasons. . . ."

"Please, President. I thought a long time before I asked you this question."

"Well, son, I don't know how to answer you. Of course, I'm trying to live a godly life. But I don't think anyone knows if he will be acceptable until he actually gets to that point."

"Oh."

"No, to answer you straight out, I don't know. I'm just doing the best I can."

"Yeah. Well, thanks, President. I'm sorry I bothered

you." I was disappointed by his response and knew it was obvious.

"No problem, son. Listen—" He paused. Then, looking into my eyes, he lifted his shoulders in a gesture of resignation. After a moment of silence, I turned slowly and walked away, wondering if I would continue in full activity in the Church for seventy years without ever having any greater sense of worthiness.[1]

Picking up *Good News for Modern Man* again, I continued to read. Something about this moment was special. I wanted more than anything to get right with God. As a Mormon, I knew that that meant I had to become righteous. If I could become good enough by living the laws and ordinances of Mormonism, then I would someday be acceptable to God. But what I was reading in Romans 1 indicated there was a way by which man could be made right with God apart from works.

In chapter three I read that no one was righteous in himself. No one was good. No one ever completely obeyed God. And Romans 3:20 said no one could ever be made right in God's sight by doing what the Law commanded. But if no one could be declared righteous that way, I thought, then how *did* one get right?

Verses 21-22 answered my question. They made clear that God's way of putting people right with Himself had

---

[1] The Celestial Kingdom is the highest of the three Mormon heavens. The other two Kingdoms are the Terrestrial and Telestial. The Terrestrial Kingdom is for people who die without Mormonism, but who embrace the truth of Mormonism in a spirit world after death. The Telestial Kingdom is the lowest "heaven." It is for people who never accept the gospel. There is also "Outer Darkness," which is reserved for Satan, his angels and people who are apostate Mormons. (Taken from *Doctrine and Covenants*, Section 88: verses 51-54; 71-75; 81-82; 35.)

nothing to do with obedience to the Law. The Bible seemed
to say that God made people right through their faith in
Jesus Christ. And verse 28 added:

> We conclude that a person is put right with God
> only through faith, and not by doing what the Law
> commands.

I shook my head in disbelief. Paul's words were destroy-
ing ten years of Mormon indoctrination. Salvation by grace
through faith!

I had heard of that concept, but I believed it was a doctrine made up by people who wanted to avoid trying to live
righteously. These chapters in Romans were telling me now
that we in the Church had put the cart before the horse—
that when I turned my life over to Christ He accepted me,
just as I was! And He dwelt in me by the Holy Spirit, who
would clean me from the inside out.

Mormonism was trying to get men clean first, by their
own efforts, in order to be acceptable to God. But the Bible
said that could never happen. Man is a hopeless sinner
whom God makes righteous immediately by faith. Then He
makes that inner cleanliness outward, in His own time.

I was reeling under what I was reading. An excitement
was also gripping me. I felt that, in some way I didn't fully
understand, I was being released from spiritual bondage.

I read eight chapters of Romans that night. The book
hammered relentlessly at the idea of salvation by good
works. When I had finished, I was absolutely different from
when I began. I was changed, renewed. I knew I was a real
Christian. And I knew that I was fully acceptable to God
because of my faith in Jesus Christ. I knew my life would
never again be the same.

As the light dawned on me, I was overwhelmed. The

condescension of it—God taking my sin! God receiving me just as I was! I believed what I read. I received it with joy. I was clean before God.

That did not answer for me all my questions about Mormonism. And aside from these, I still believed Joseph Smith was a prophet and that the Book of Mormon was true. But I knew I had found my peace with God.

In my elation, I did not realize that peace was soon to be shattered. Jesus said He had come not to bring peace, but a sword—a sword that separates families.

That sword, for me, was now unsheathed.

12

THE SWORD OF DIVISION

I tend to be the dreamer in our family, Margaretta the nose-to-the-grindstone person. My new ideas and good-natured optimism often lead us into some interesting, even painful situations. Now, I knew, Margaretta wasn't about to listen to any unconventional ideas about religion. So as yet, I said nothing to her about my experience in the book of Romans.

I did, on the other hand, want to share my experience with my friend Fred Johnson. My chance came several weeks after I became a Christian, when a miraculous chain of events led me to Wyoming on business. I left on a Friday morning for the weekend. I called Fred and made arrangements to stay with his family and talk with him and his father, Stan.

Arriving in Basin Saturday night, I joined Fred and Stan around Fred's kitchen table. They were excited for me as I recounted my conversion experience with enthusiasm. Then we discussed what I should do about my affiliation with the Mormon Church.

"Whether or not you remain a member of the Mormon Church is not really the issue, Jim," said Stan over a cup of coffee. "The point is, you will need strong Christian fellowship."

"I know that already. I can't get enough of the Bible!"

Fred reached over and touched my hand. "Remember, you're going to have to be charitable toward Margaretta and your friends. You need to move slowly."

I took a sip of coffee. "What do you think I ought to do about leaving the Church?"

"I think that's going to take care of itself, Jim," said Stan. "Probably sooner than you realize. You're going to go through some things you won't like. Your faith will be tested."

We talked until nearly dawn, praying for guidance, patience and understanding. I resolved to give up my teaching position in the Church.

The next morning the three of us attended their small Baptist church, where I found myself in my first actual church service since my conversion. As I listened to the hymns and preaching, I began again to weep. I didn't know why sobs shook my two hundred-plus pound frame, except that as the preacher spoke I saw for the first time the heart of my loving God. I saw my sin and rebellion contrasted with God's gracious, forgiving nature. I experienced the cleansing and acceptance that comes with repentance.

After the service I stood outside looking at the ground, trying not to attract attention, but the tears wouldn't stop flowing. Over lunch with Fred, I got myself together emotionally. But afterward my eyes began to fill up, and I found myself unable to speak. When I pointed to my car, Fred squeezed my hand, nodding understandingly, and I got in without saying goodbye.

Driving home that night across the isolation of the Wyoming Rockies, the stars looked like dancing diamonds in the black void above. I listened to at least half-a-dozen radio evangelists and preachers on the clear channel stations of the West. As I listened, an incredible thought struck me: All these speakers were preaching the same message!

I don't mean they spoke on exactly the same subject, but the common thread was salvation by faith in Jesus Christ. I realized there is a simple message of salvation that pervades Christian preaching. That surprised me, since I had been taught that the formation of different denominations proved that people could not agree doctrinally. But the evangelists I heard seemed to represent the same God with the same message, speaking almost with one voice.

Once back home in St. Anthony, I set about to look for a Christian bookstore. I found a small one in Idaho Falls. The entire store was housed in a twenty-by-twenty back room off a Christian coffeehouse.

When I introduced myself to the owner and told her I was a born-again Mormon elder, she nearly dropped the stack of books she was trying to shelve. Dorothy was well-acquainted with Mormonism and trying to make a go of the only Christian bookstore in Idaho Falls, a city of 50,000 serving a potential market of 150,000. So she appreciated my unique position, and invited me to a Bible study later that night in a home in Idaho Falls. I promised to be there.

I arrived to find the meeting already underway. The house was packed! Thirty people stood in a circle singing Scripture choruses. They made a space for me and I tried to follow the singing. After a while someone began to pray, while others interjected comments: *Amen. Hallelujah. Thank You, Jesus.*

Later I was introduced to the group. Dorothy had told them about me before I arrived. They said they had been praying for me and for my family. After the meeting I asked the two "elders" in charge, Dewey Wilmot and Ben Lunis, to pray for me. Their prayer made me cry again, of course! I felt so close to God. And for that matter, I noticed that Dewey and Ben had gotten teary-eyed, too. Then I saw that twenty people were watching and they, too, were crying. I went home floating on a cloud of joy.

By Sunday morning I was so confident of the power of God in my life that I got up early and drove twelve miles to Rexburg for an early church service. There, Mike Shaw pastored a second Presbyterian church, in addition to the Community Church in St. Anthony where I had met him; and I preferred going to church out-of-town where no one knew me. Afterward I hurried back for my gospel doctrine class at Fourth Ward. I knew Margaretta wouldn't suspect anything, since I often went out for a solitary drive to prepare my lesson.

That morning my class got something a little different: I read aloud the first eight chapters of Romans from *Good News for Modern Man*. That was a radical departure from the way we usually did things! Normally we followed a lesson outline and skipped through the Bible, picking and choosing texts to support our theme. No one was accustomed to hearing such a lengthy portion of Scripture.

Nor did my class seem to feel the same way I did about this particular passage. When I finished reading and looked up, I saw a congregation of crossed arms and icy stares. Surprised but undaunted, I wound up the class by saying, "I know that many of you are hurting in a lot of ways. Some of you think you are not good enough for God to even care about. But I want you to know that Jesus loves you very much. There is nothing too big for Him to handle in your life. You need to quit striving to please Him and just allow yourself to be accepted by Him. You need to turn your heart over to Him."

When I finished speaking, silence reigned. At last one of

the women, a little more outspoken than the rest, said in disdain, "What you are saying this morning sounds like something Billy Graham would say—'Just give your heart to Jesus and everything will be all right!'"

I looked at her incredulously and said, "I guess that's what I *am* saying."

After the meeting I went up to the Sunday school superintendent. "I won't be teaching this class anymore. I want you to get someone else as soon as you can."

"What's the matter, Jim?" he asked.

"Nothing," I replied. "I just want to let someone else have the privilege for a while."

Margaretta must have gotten wind of the goings-on at church. Outside in the car she said sharply, "I want to talk to you!"

"What about?" I replied weakly.

"You've left the Church, haven't you?" I detected fierceness in her tone.

"Well. . . ."

"*Haven't* you?" she demanded.

"Well, not exactly."

"I told you if you ever left the Church, we were through! I married a Mormon elder. My little girl's father is a Mormon elder. If you are not a Mormon elder, you are not my husband—or Erin's father!"

We rode home in silence. I was sure she would get over being angry and I could reason with her.

But when we got home, she started packing my clothes. I followed her around protesting, but it dawned on me that she was serious. Then she threw my clothes out the front door, shoved me out the door, and slammed and locked it.

I felt like a fool standing on the step. I was feeling something else, too—a cold wave of fear. She was dead serious!

Margaretta and I had been married for seven years. We had had our problems, but I saw something different in her that day. One thing I knew about Margaretta: she never bluffed. I had the option of fitting in or saying goodbye to our marriage.

I wasn't sure what to do. Reasoning with her was out of the question. At least, it was right then. Maybe by morning. I needed to let her get things straightened out in her mind.

I drove aimlessly around for awhile, then stopped by the Community Church to talk with Mike. I hoped he would have a solution for me, but his face was ashen as he listened to my story.

Mike was not as naive as I. He had pastored in that Mormon town for some time. He had tried to fit in with the Mormons, to regard them as brothers. For a number of years he had even held joint community Thanksgiving services with them. But he had slowly, reluctantly concluded that there was no basis for fellowship with them. "Jim," he had said to me (before I was able to understand), "I simply do not worship the same God the Mormons do."

Mike was not very encouraging. He was realistic.

I decided to stay the night with a friend and call Margaretta in the morning.

The next day was worse. Margaretta was immovable. "You need to be very certain your new religion is worth what it's going to cost you," she told me.

She agreed to meet that evening to talk things over. I promised not to make any trouble. She said I was not coming home until I changed my position. I could come over and talk, but I was not moving back in.

We talked in the bathroom with the door closed so we would not confuse six-year-old Erin, who was being taught good Mormon doctrine. Margaretta sat on the edge of the tub and cried as she told me how impossible the situation was.

"All my life," she said, "the only thing I wanted was to be

married in the temple and have a husband who was true to the Church. I haven't made tremendous demands on you, but I can't give in to this.

"It's so embarrassing for me," she continued bitterly. "Everyone is looking at me. My parents are crushed. And you—you walk around not caring how I feel!"

"It isn't that I don't care," I said. "It's that I don't have any choice. Something has happened to me. I've been born again. I'm saved. I have to follow Jesus. I can't turn back."

"What does *that* mean?" she asked through a tissue.

"It means that I'm right with God. I'm forgiven. I'm going to heaven."

"You can't possibly know that!"

"But I do know it. My sins have been forgiven."

"Oh, I know," she said sarcastically. "Your sins are forgiven. That means that no matter what you do, you're still going to heaven."

"That's sort of the idea," I said. "But there's more to it than that."

"I suppose if you committed murder you would still go to heaven."

"If I repented. If I was really sorry."

"Oh, this is so pointless," she said. "The real problem is that you don't care how all this looks. What about me? What about Erin? How is she going to have any respect in this town when her father is some kind of kooky Christian?"

"Margaretta," I said, "I don't have any choice. I have decided to follow Jesus and I can't go back. There must be some way we can work this out."

"There isn't, unless you change."

"I can't."

"Well, neither can I," she said, standing up.

As she walked out of the bathroom she said soberly, "Jim, I'm telling you to give up this foolishness or you are going to lose everything that's dear to you."

As ı pondered her words, I was engulfed in a hope-lessness like nothing I had ever known. There seemed no way out.

When I called her a few days later, she told me she had seen a lawyer. He was a Mormon and he told her there probably was no solution. Divorce was imminent.

The next few weeks in early 1974 were the worst I had ever experienced. I had stopped going to church at Fourth Ward. I was living alone, my heart tearing from the roots. Seeing pictures of myself visiting with Erin, my little blonde angel, on weekends in the park. I had to pray just for enough energy to walk across the room.

No one understood how I felt. My Mormon friends thought I was crazy. My non-Mormon, non-Christian friends thought I was crazy, too. "Listen, Jim," said one of them. "You can believe anything you want, but go back home and be a good Mormon. Who will know the differ-ence?"

My new Christian friends understood why I could not go back, but I'm not sure anyone could understand what I was feeling.

"Surely, God," I pleaded, "this is not what You want. You don't want me to lose my family. What do You want me to do?"

Follow Me, was His reply.

"But what about my family?"

Your family is My concern. You must follow Me.

"But at least promise me that someday I'll get my family back."

I don't make deals. You must simply follow Me. There are no group plans, no fleet rates. This is an individual matter. Margaret-ta and Erin are not your concern. They are My concern. Can you leave them in My hands?

"Does that mean that Margaretta may divorce me?"

She may. She is free to do what she will. I compel no one to come. I only draw. She will have to decide for herself.

On the telephone, Margaretta was growing harder, more distant. All her friends and family were convinced that the best thing for everyone was to let me go my own crazy way, and to simply divorce me.

As for me, the die was cast. There was no turning back. The words of one of the songs we sang in Bible study kept echoing in my ears:

> I have decided to follow Jesus.
> I have decided to follow Jesus.
> I have decided to follow Jesus.
> No turning back,
> No turning back.

13

A REPRIEVE

Realistically, there was only one course of action open to Margaretta. From childhood she had been prepared to marry in the temple. The Church teaches its children to perpetuate the Mormon family. Little boys grow up singing "I Hope They Call Me on a Mission." And little girls are tucked in with stories about being married in the temple.

For the Mormon, family life actually starts in heaven. The Church teaches that we were not created at birth, but that we were "spirit children of Heavenly Father and Mother." We are the spirit brothers and sisters of Jesus and, for that matter, Satan![1]

The best of the spirit children are born to parents who have been "sealed" in the temple. If you are not sealed to your family in this life, you will not be with them in heaven.

---

[1] Mormon theology gets a little messy here, for although Mormonism teaches that humans were born as "spirit children," the Church teaches just as clearly that we are "co-eternal" with God. Joseph Smith said we existed from the beginning with God.

Since I had left the Church, I could not, of course, go to the Celestial Kingdom. Margaretta was forced, therefore, to choose between her husband and heaven. Who, I asked myself, could take that kind of pressure?

Mormon society puts young women under all kinds of pressure. In Utah, for example, girls marry as teenagers twice as frequently as in the nation as a whole.[2] And the Mormon birth rate is twice the national average.[3] Women are encouraged to marry young and create bodies for spirit children. Interestingly, more than half the teenagers who marry in Utah are pregnant out-of-wedlock![4]

So I knew, as torn as I felt inside, that Margaretta must feel equally torn, and even abandoned. She had been spoon-fed since birth the idea that all but Mormonism was corrupt. One of the original twelve Mormon apostles, Orson Pratt, had put it this way:

> All other churches are entirely destitute of all authority from God. . . . Both Catholics and Protestants are nothing less than the 'whore of Babylon.' . . . Any person to be so wicked as to receive a holy ordinance from the ministers of any of these apostate churches will be sent down to hell with them unless they repent. . . . [5]

The Church makes no apologies for its narrow view. Joseph Smith said that God told him that all the churches of

---

[2] *Ogden Standard-Examiner,* December 15, 1979.

[3] *Statistical Abstract of the United States,* 1981-82, p. 60.

[4] *Ogden Standard-Examiner,* December 15, 1979.

[5] *Seer,* Orson Pratt, p. 225.

that day "were wrong, *all* their creeds were abominations and *all* their members were corrupt."[6]

Margaretta, as a faithful Mormon, believed the Church to be the only representative of God on earth. And now she found herself married to a man who had been misled by the devil. It was no wonder she had told me, through tears of frustration, "I hate the people who have done this to you!"

For myself, I had just about given up on the future of our marriage. The last time I had called Margaretta, she had given me no shred of hope.

Nevertheless, one day at work I decided to call her one more time. I was surprised by what she said. We could talk! Would I be willing to meet with her and the stake president to see if there were any way to avoid a divorce?

Of course, I agreed to the meeting. I knew I could not compromise my decision for Christ, but short of that I was willing to agree to any reasonable request. I wondered if it would be possible to find a way through this thicket of division.

President Jones met us at the door, shook my hand warmly and ushered us into his office. He waved me into a folding chair, seated Margaretta next to me, and took his place behind his desk. I had known President Jones for some years, had done business with him and was very fond of him. He was a small man who moved with quick, nervous motions.

Clearing his throat, he straightened his shoulders within his dark brown suit jacket. "Well, Brother Spencer, I'm glad you were willing to meet with me."

"I'm very glad for the chance to talk to you."

---

[6] *Pearl of Great Price,* Joseph Smith, 2:18-19.

"I want you to know, Jim, that I am not in favor of you and Margaretta getting a divorce."

That statement surprised me, since in the conversations I had had with Margaretta, I had gotten the impression that no one thought she should continue to live with me if I left the Church.

"I'm sure glad to hear that, President. I don't want a divorce!"

He nodded and adjusted his wire-rimmed glasses. "Of course, Jim, as you know, you have presented Margaretta with an impossible situation. You know that her reputation in the community has suffered greatly from what you have done, not to say the fact that you are endangering her spiritual future."

I ignored the last part of his remark. "I really don't want to disgrace her in the community, President."

"I'm sure you don't. Tell me, Brother Spencer"—reverting to the more formal form of address—"what *really* is the problem you are having with the Church?"

"Basically my problems are doctrinal. I have come to believe, after much soul-searching, that the Church is in error in several important positions."

"Are you sure that's all that's bothering you? Has someone offended you in some way?"

"Absolutely not. I love the people in Fourth Ward. My problem is that I have lost confidence in the Church. I can't accept some of the things the Church teaches. For example, plurality of gods."

"What about Joseph Smith? Do you think he was a prophet? What about the Book of Mormon?"

"President, I'm not sure what I believe there. But even if the Book of Mormon is true and even if Joseph Smith was a prophet, that doesn't mean the Church today is sound."

President Jones looked troubled. "What about plurality

of gods? What's your problem? The prophets have told us, 'As man is, God once was; and as God is, man may become.'"

"I know what the prophets have said. I just don't agree with them."

"What *do* you believe?"

"I believe there is only one God. I believe what the Bible says—that in all the universe there is only one God."

President Jones laughed. "How can you believe that? Joseph Smith saw two personages in the Palmyra grove—two separate, distinct personages!"

"Maybe."

"All right. If you discount the word of the prophet, what about the Bible? You do believe in the Bible, don't you?"

"I most certainly do. I believe in the God of the Bible and I believe that Jesus is God, the God who came in the flesh."

"So you think Jesus is God?"

"Yes, I do."

"What about God the Father?"

"The Bible says that Jesus and the Father are one. Jesus said in John 14:9, 'He who has seen me has seen the Father.'"

"Of course that means that the Father and the Son are one in *purpose*," responded President Jones. "You don't actually think they are the same Being, do you?"

"Yes, I do."

"Then how do you account for the fact that Jesus, when He was in the Garden of Gethsemane, prayed to the Father? Or the fact that at the baptism of Jesus, the Spirit descended as a dove and the Father said from heaven, 'This is my beloved Son'?"

"I'm not sure I fully understand. But even if I don't, I believe the Bible. And the Bible tells me there is only one God. Here, let me read you a couple of verses."

President Jones looked irritated. He was supposed to be the spiritual authority here. "Well—" he began.

"No, let me finish, President. Here it is, Isaiah 44:6. God says, 'I am the first and I am the last; besides me there is no god.'"

"Well, we believe there is only one God *for this world*."

"I know what the Church teaches, but that isn't what God says in the Bible. Listen to Isaiah 44:8: 'You are my witnesses! Is there a God besides me? There is no Rock; I know not any.' See, God says He doesn't know of any other god. Don't you think if there were other gods in the universe He would know about them?"

President Jones was beginning to scowl.

"Here's another verse, Isaiah 45:5. 'I am the Lord, and there is no other, besides me there is no God; I gird you . . . that men may know, from the rising of the sun and from the west, that there is none besides me; I am the Lord, and there is no other.'"

"I think that's enough verses, Jim."

"The point I'm trying to make, President, is that the idea of plurality of gods, as taught by the Church, does not line up with the Bible. Now, I can't explain the Trinity, President Jones. I believe there is only one God because the Bible says that's all there is. Yet somehow, within the nature of that one God, are three Persons. That's the doctrine of the Trinity— one God, three Persons.

"I don't know how God can be both three and one, but I know that's the clear teaching of the complete witness of the Old and New Testaments. God is one, but He continually displays three eternal Persons to us—Father, Son and Holy Spirit. Even the Book of Mormon teaches that the Father and the Son are the same being."

"Nonsense!"

"No, it's true. Mosiah chapter seven, verse 27 says that

Christ is God, the Father of all things, and that He came down and took upon Himself the image of a man!"

"Well—"

"And Mosiah 16:15 says that Christ is 'the very Eternal Father.' So does Alma 11:38. And Third Nephi 11:36 says the Father and the Son, along with the Holy Ghost, are one. And the *Doctrine and Covenants*—"[7]

"O.K., Jim, that's enough!"

"President, I don't understand all these things, but this much I do know. There's a vast difference between what the Bible says about God and the Church's concept that every faithful male member can become God! Even if there were three gods—Father, Son and Holy Ghost—there are not millions of gods, and you and I are not going to be gods!

"And the idea of God having once been a man who grew into godhood is nowhere in the Bible. As a matter of fact, it isn't even in the Book of Mormon. I wrote down this verse, Mormon 9:9-10: 'For do we not read that God is the same yesterday, today and forever, and in him there is no variableness, neither shadow of changing? And now if ye have imagined up unto yourselves a god who doth vary, and in whom there is shadow of changing, then ye imagined up unto yourselves a god who is not a God of miracles.' President, a god who grew from manhood into Godhood is a god who has changed. He is neither the God of the Bible nor of the Book of Mormon. Furthermore—"

"I said that's enough, Jim." President Jones looked down at his hands, folded tightly in front of him. "I don't know how to respond to you, Jim." Then looking me in the eye: "As a matter of fact, I'm not really a Bible scholar. But I have a testimony of the gospel. I know that Joseph Smith was a

---

[7] See also Book of Mormon: Alma 11:26-32; III Nephi 11:27; Mormon 9:12; Ether 3:14; and *Doctrine and Covenants*, Section 20.28.

prophet; that this is the True Church; and that we have a living prophet at the head of the Church today!" He was as close to being angry as I had ever seen him.

"But beyond that, Jim," he continued more calmly, "what are we going to do about your marriage? Your wife must be married to a Mormon elder in order to go to the Celestial Kingdom. She told me that all her life she had hoped to be married in the temple. You took her to the temple, Jim! Now what are you going to do? Abandon her?"

Margaretta had been silent all along. I looked at her now. She was staring at the president. I thought she looked disappointed, and particularly so when he had confessed that he was not a Bible student. I wondered what was going through her mind. Then I looked back at President Jones. "The fact is, President, she *is* my wife."

"Yes. And I, for one, do not want to see your marriage end. But you are going to have to cooperate, or I'm not going to be able to help you. Do you understand?"

"Yes, sir, I do. But *you* need to understand that I have struggled with this a long time. I am not moving capriciously. There are compromises I cannot make."

"I'm willing to respect that, Jim. I think we need to come up with a compromise that will be a step toward bringing your marriage together. I have a suggestion. Why don't you take the missionary lessons?"

I smiled wearily. "President, I have *given* the missionary lessons. I know what they are. I just don't believe them."

"Yes, well. . . . Look, Jim, we need to find some common ground here. What would you say to reading the Book of Mormon?"

"I guess I could do that. But a compromise should give a little on both sides. If we're going to try to think things through, shouldn't Margaretta be involved in some way?"

"I think that's fair. Maybe Margaretta can read—" He paused, groping. "Maybe she can read the Bible."

"Well, President, I don't see how that's fair. She's already supposed to believe in the Bible. I tell you what. I'll read the Book of Mormon again if you will tell her to read some books that I'll give her."

"No! No, I—uh—I don't think that would be right." He closed his eyes and paused reflectively. "How about this? How about if you both traded off going to church together?"

"What do you mean?" I asked slowly.

"Well, you go to church with her at Fourth Ward one Sunday, and let her go to church with you, wherever you go, the next Sunday!"

Nothing he could have said would have surprised me more. I couldn't believe my ears. Before he had time to reconsider I said, "Well, O.K. I think that would be all right." Turning to Margaretta, I could see fire in her eyes. "What do you think, honey?"

Margaretta glared at me. Then she looked icily at President Jones. "Are you sure that's the right thing to do?"

"Well, now, dear, I understand that we're asking a lot of you. But I have complete confidence in your faithfulness and I think we need to give Jim a little more room. I'm confident that eventually he's going to realize how serious a step he is taking."

"I certainly hope so! I can guarantee you one thing. I'm not about to leave the Church. I'm not about to become a—a Presbyterian!"

President Jones rose to his feet. The interview was over, an unpleasant job well done. He smiled again and walked us to the door. "I just know things will work out. Get back with me in a few weeks and let me know what's happening."

We found ourselves outside the building, standing in nervous silence. Was I to go home with her or return to my bachelor quarters? Finally Margaretta sighed and started walking to the car. "Come on," she called over her shoulder.

I felt great. I didn't really know why, but I was actually going home! It was no time to ask questions.

14

SORTING OUT

Margaretta and I fell into an uneasy peace. We did alternate going to church together. But beyond that, we did not discuss our religious differences.

I continued my search for truth, feeling an urgency to uncover the roots of Mormonism. It was important, I felt, to find out where I had gone wrong. I hoped understanding might eventually lead to deliverance for Margaretta, too. So night after night, usually after she and Erin were in bed, I pored over books and papers on the kitchen table.

To understand Mormonism, I knew I first had to understand Joseph Smith. The Church teaches that Mormonism stands or falls with the prophet Joseph. For Mormons, he was the innocent fourteen-year-old farm boy praying about which church to join, who was suddenly confronted by God and directed to "restore the True Church."

Yet Mormonism produced polygamy and polytheism— backward steps in civilization. And it produced a monolithic hierarchy which has bred social problems that discourage sociologists.[1] The more I studied, the more I realized that Mormonism undermines the entire structure of orthodox Christianity.

What had gone wrong? How could Joseph have gotten so far off base? Worse, how could so many people follow him? How could *I* have followed him? And could answering these questions help to change anything?

Joseph Smith claimed to be a prophet. I soon discovered that his claim was not unique. In America, prophets are numerous. And of the many American religions they have started in the last two hundred years, some remain sizable, like Smith's Mormonism, Mary Baker Eddy's Christian Science, and Charles Taze Russell's Jehovah's Witnesses.

The Presbyterian evangelist Charles Finney referred to Joseph Smith's upper New York State as the "burned-over district" because of the variety and intensity of religious fervor there. The area was called a "psychic highway" and looked upon by orthodox churchmen as a hotbed of "ultraism" where settlers brought with them an experimental approach to religious and social ideas. Contemporaries of Smith germinated such movements as Shakerism, spiritualism and the sexual communism of the Oneida community.[2]

How, I asked myself, could one judge a man who claimed to be a prophet? When someone like Joseph Smith claimed to be sent from God, how did one determine if he was acting on his own or on God's behalf?

When presented with a choice between Joseph Smith and the apostle Paul, I had chosen instinctively to believe

---

[1] Gerald Smith, a caseworker with the Child Welfare Unit in Salt Lake County, says of child abuse in Utah, "I'm just blackly pessimistic about it. Lack of maturity and selfishness are pandemic" (The *Idaho Falls Post-Register*, June 27, 1982).

[2] *Eerdman's Handbook to Christianity in America*, pp. 174-175.

the Bible. But why? Were there any reasonable grounds for my doing that?

I knew, of course, that the Mormon Church undermined the authority of the Bible. Our Eighth Article of Faith read:

> We believe the Bible to be the Word of God insofar as it is translated correctly. We also believe the Book of Mormon to be the Word of God.

Joseph Smith was fond of saying, when he came across something in the Bible he didn't like, that "an old Jew without any authority" changed the Scripture.[3] And Mormon apostle Orson Pratt published a pamphlet in the 1850s called *The Bible Alone: An Insufficient Guide,* in which he wrote:

> What evidence have they [Protestants] that the Book of Matthew was inspired of God, or any of the books of the New Testament?[4]

The Mormon Church maintained that the Bible was unreliable, and that we needed a prophet to straighten out the confusion. Such a prophet would disregard previous revelation and speak whatever he would as Scripture. Brigham Young had stated:

> I have never preached a sermon and sent it out to the children of men, that they cannot call Scripture. Let me have a privilege of correcting a sermon, and it's as good a Scripture as they deserve.[5]

---

[3] *Journal of Discourses,* Joseph Smith, Vol. 6, p. 4.

[4] *Orson Pratt's Works,* Orson Pratt, pp. 44-47.

[5] *Journal of Discourses,* Vol. 13, p. 95.

Mormonism, in its claim to be the only True Church, and despite its claim that Jesus was the Christ, had cut itself off completely from Christianity. Joseph Smith had declared that there was no spiritual representative on earth until he came along, and that all other religions were evil. He said that all other priests and their followers, "without one exception, receive their portion with the devil and his angels."[6]

Orson Pratt went further. He called Christianity the work of the devil—"a perfect pack of nonsense . . . corrupt as hell. . . ."[7]

I also found in my studies that, as Joseph Smith had pitted his revelation against the Bible, orthodox Christianity agreed unanimously that the Mormon Church was a non-Christian cult. According to *The New International Dictionary of the Christian Church*, for instance, "The doctrines taught by the Mormon Church deny most of the cardinal points of the Christian Church."[8]

By the same token, the rest of the world, Jew or Gentile, secular or Christian, declared categorically that the text of the Bible was accurate.[9] Through the science of textual criticism, supported by thousands of Scripture fragments and the Dead Sea Scrolls, we could be sure that we possessed, preserved with minute accuracy, what the apostles John and Paul and others actually wrote.

---

[6] *The Elder's Journal*, Vol. 4, pp. 59-60.

[7] *Journal of Discourses*, Vol. 6, p. 167.

[8] *New International Dictionary of the Christian Church* (Zondervan Publishing House, Grand Rapids, Mich.), p. 678.

[9] For a good documentation of textual criticism of the Bible for laymen, I recommend *Evidence that Demands a Verdict*, Josh McDowell (Campus Crusade for Christ, International).

Joseph Smith wanted to have his cake and eat it, too. He wanted to be a prophet of the God of the Bible, yet he wanted to throw out the Bible. To me, it wouldn't wash.

At some point in Joseph's ministry, he penned the Eighth Article of Faith in an attempt to cover himself by discrediting the Bible. By taking that position he was saying, in effect, "When the Bible agrees with me, it is right. When it disagrees with me, it is wrong."

In addition to discrediting the Bible, Joseph proposed the concept of plurality of gods.[10] The idea that men could become gods had bothered me from the first time I heard it in priesthood class shortly after I joined the Church. Polytheism—the belief in the existence of more than one god—was the bedrock issue of Mormonism. The more I studied, the more I concluded that polytheism was Mormonism's basic error.

Joseph Smith not only believed and taught polytheism; he even boasted about it. He claimed to have always preached plurality of gods, and he told his congregation, "You have got to learn how to be Gods yourselves . . . the same as all Gods have done before you . . . until you are able to dwell in everlasting burnings and to sit in glory."[11]

Brigham Young embellished Joseph's theory, saying: "Man is King of Kings and Lord of Lords in embryo."[12]

Some Christians I had spoken with were surprised to hear that the Mormon Church taught such things. I made clear to them that Mormon polytheism was not some deep, dark truth that only a privileged few Mormons mutter to

---

[10]*Documented History of the Church*, Vol. 6, p. 474.

[11]*Journal of Discourses*. Vol. 6, p. 4.

[12]*Journal of Discourses*, Vol. 10, p. 223.

each other in the tops of the temples. This polytheistic doctrine was believed by every serious Mormon.

The Bible taught from cover to cover, on the other hand, that there was only one God. This belief in monotheism was the cornerstone of all Judeo-Christian thought. (See Appendix A: *Monotheism.)*

As I cried out to God for knowledge and understanding, I came to see that all occult "revelation" ultimately produced polytheism. Every false religion attempted to de-deify God and to deify man. Christian Science told us to discover our own "Christ-consciousness." Jehovah's Witnesses told us that Jesus was "another God."

At the same time, I suspected that polytheism was packaged more successfully in Mormonism than in any other contemporary Western religion. In Mormonism as nowhere else, the lie of the deceiver in the Garden was subtly perpetrated: "Don't listen to God. Listen to me and you will become like God."

The more I studied—sometimes late into the night—the more I discovered that Mormonism was a contradictory maze from beginning to end. Mormon prophets contradicted each other as well as the Book of Mormon and other Latter-day "revelation." Mormon revelation was not, as the Church claimed, a clear stream of truth revealing God's will for man, but a sinuous river of dark backwaters and bottomless whirlpools. (See Appendix B: *Confusion Among the Prophets.)*

I learned, for instance, that Mormon history was marked by controversy and cover-ups. The web of confusion of Mormonism was so complete that, to preserve his sanity, the faithful Mormon was forced (if he were to remain faithful) to accept the *current* position of the Church on any given matter. Truth was what Salt Lake City said it was on a particular day.

Apparently nothing in Mormonism was too sacred to change. The Fourteen Articles of Faith had been changed to the Thirteen Articles of Faith. Polygamy was introduced, defended, then set aside. Entire sections of the *Doctrine and Covenants* had been rewritten. And the Book of Mormon, called the most perfect and error-free book ever produced, had been altered in nearly 4,000 places since the 1830 edition. (See Appendix C: *Changes in the Book of Mormon.*) The Church had even "re-edited" Joseph Smith's mother's biography of the prophet.

I found that the study of change and false prophecy in the Church was boundless, ranging from the sublime to the ridiculous. In one statement, for example, Joseph Smith said that the inhabitants of the moon were tall, about six feet, dressed in the style of Quakers and lived to be about a thousand years old.[13]

Brigham Young said that men inhabited not only the moon, but also the sun.[14]

Joseph prophesied that Jesus would return by 1891.[15]

Brigham declared that the Civil War would not free the slaves.[16]

Some of the things the Church asked the faithful to believe bordered on insanity. Brigham Young said the earth was alive.[17]

Orson Pratt said that before men and women are born on earth as babies, their spirits are adult-sized in heaven. When they are born, their spirits are compressed, which

---

[13]*The Young Woman's Journal*, Vol. 3, p. 262.

[14]*Journal of Discourses*, Vol. 13, p. 271.

[15]*History of the Church*, Vol. 2, p. 182.

[16]*Journal of Discourses*, Vol. 10, p. 250.

[17]*Journal of Discourses*, Vol. 6, p. 36.

causes a loss of memory.[18] He also said vegetables have spirits, are the offspring of male and female vegetable spirits, and are capable of being happy.[19]

As I looked at the contradictions and confusion, alterations and prevarications that went into the mix of Mormonism, I marveled that anyone could believe the doctrine. I marveled even more that I had not only believed but taught it.

Often in these late-night sessions I would put my head down on the table and pray, thanking God for cutting through the confusion, and praying He would do so soon for Margaretta and Erin.

As I reviewed my experience in Mormonism, I recognized the deep forces that had worked on me. When I joined the Mormon Church, recently out of the Navy and hungry for meaning in my life, I had longed for love and acceptance. Presented with the clean orderliness of Mormonism, I had made a conscious decision to alter my lifestyle drastically in order to gain that acceptance. I wanted to be "in."

Such a desire for acceptance, I learned, is what feeds people into occult religions, whether Mormonism, Moonieism or Hare Krishna. The perfect cult candidate is a young, dissatisfied idealist. For this reason, all cults try to become visible on college campuses. (Mormondom aims even younger: Practically every high school has an outreach building adjacent to school property.)

I was to learn, through psychological studies of former cult members, that a process occurs in the mind that psychologists call "snapping." Snapping occurs when subjects

---

[18]*Journal of Discourses*, Vol. 16, pp. 333-334.

[19]*The Seer*, Orson Pratt, pp. 33-34, 37-38.

are forced, in order to gain acceptance among cult members, to make a leap of faith requiring them to discard their question-asking mechanism. They are compelled to put their minds on the shelf, at which point a basic, mind-altering experience occurs. (See Appendix D: *Psychological "Snapping" in the Cults.)*

When I met the Mormon missionaries, I was searching for personal fulfillment. And in order to be accepted, I was willing to make decisions that gave the Church control over my mind.

When I had first heard the statement in my priesthood class, "As man is, God once was; as God is, man may become," I was shocked. My conscience rose up against the blasphemy. And at that instant I had a decision to make: Either I would listen to my God-given conscience, or I would submit to the authority of the cult.

For one instant in that priesthood class, my conscience had asserted itself. *No,* I had cried out within myself. *That's blasphemy. I will never be God!* But I wanted acceptance. After Ed explained that this was Joseph Smith's revelation, and when he pressured me to accept the teaching, I made a potentially fatal decision: I capitulated. I accepted what I instinctively knew to be false because the price of resistance was too high. I bought into the concept that there was no essential difference between God and man, and in so doing violated my conscience.

Likewise, my first trip to the temple had revulsed me. But by the seventh trip, my revulsion was only light nausea. Much later, as I read the temple ceremony, I would be overwhelmed that I had participated in high-level occult prayer circles with signs, symbols, secret handshakes and blood oaths. I had stood mutely by and observed temple plays in which Christian pastors were portrayed as Satan's dupes.

What I had really done was to exercise my freedom of choice at the expense of my conscience. I had violated something innate, something the apostle Paul says is born within every man—the knowledge of the Creator God. My heart had become darkened, and I had "exchanged the glory of the immortal God for images resembling mortal man" (Romans 1:23).

Such violations had led me on a path away from light and into darkness, spiraling downward into the black confusion of the world of the cult. Each time I made such a decision, I gave up part of my humanity. I sold part of my heritage for acceptance in the cult. I took part of my mind, created in the image of God, and put it in a plastic bag and placed it on a shelf.

I could now clearly see that Mormonism was, as Dr. Walter Martin (the foremost authority on non-Christian cults) termed it—"a polytheistic nightmare of confused doctrine masquerading as the Church of Christ."

Pushing back my chair one night and laying aside my glasses, the rest of the house dark and quiet, I got up from the kitchen table where I had been studying and went to the living room window. Outside the March night was crisp and cold. Snow still covered the streets and was piled high on the corners. I watched a car come nearly to a complete stop as it felt its way through our intersection.

I had finally worked my way free from the hold of Mormonism. I had a solid hold on the God of the Bible. I only wished Margaretta could see what I saw. But she was not receptive.

O God, I prayed, *it's so clear to those who see, yet impossible to see unless You give vision. O God, my wife and my daughter. . . .*

My prayer trailed off as I gave them over into His hands.

He gave me peace. My times were in His hands. There could be no other way.

15

EXCOMMUNICATION!

One morning several months after I had come home, I awakened to the sound of Margaretta moaning beside me in the bed. Quickly I snapped on the dressing table light. There it was again—the vacant look. The pain.

After seven years of marriage, Margaretta was carrying our second child. Almost immediately upon her decision to let me come back home, she had conceived this new life. We were elated at the prospect of another child.

But Margaretta was getting terribly morning-sick. With Erin, she had spent several weeks in bed and dropped below 100 pounds. This time was even worse.

"How ya doin', kid?" I asked.

She shook her head, then gestured frantically toward the side of the bed. I grabbed the stainless steel bowl and held it to her face. Out of her mouth came dark green bile. She retched and gripped my hand, writhing in pain, gagging. I noticed a faint pink mark radiating from the corner of her mouth where the repeated touch of the acid bile had burned her face.

This scene had played itself out several times already, and I had come to recognize this as the breaking point.

"I'm calling the hospital," I said. She didn't even attempt to reply.

On the way to the hospital, I felt the warm summer air caress my face as Margaretta leaned against the opposite door. How long could she hold up under the strain of the violent nausea accompanying her pregnancy?

At the hospital, a nurse helped her down the hall while I went to the duty desk. Another nurse, one I knew from previous visits, was already making out the admittance report.

"We'll get the I.V. going right away, Jim," she said, glancing up from her work. "Gets kind of old, doesn't it?"

Back outside, I thought of the past few months of Margaretta's pregnancy. She had been hospitalized several times in order to receive intravenous feeding, since she was acutely dehydrated. She vomited so much her face burned. Margaretta is five feet five, but by the sixth month of pregnancy, at 79 pounds, she looked like a concentration camp victim.

The doctors who attended her were confounded. Most of them believed she was either malingering or experiencing deep depression. Her Mormon doctor (and our close friend) recommended tubal ligation in order to prevent future pregnancy. His prognosis was grave.

Pastor Mike often came by to visit Margaretta. She noticed that when he sat and held her hand the pain and nausea abated, and as soon as he left, the illness returned. Rich Laux, a Missouri Synod Lutheran pastor, would also visit. And Dewey Wilmot from the Idaho Falls prayer group often drove up to pray for her. Margaretta received these men with reservations; she was polite but distant. There were no openings.

One day George Eichler, pastor of a local Southern Baptist church, stopped by. George was quiet, almost shy. Even though we did not attend his church, he took a special interest in us.

Now, George took Margaretta's hand. "Dear," he smiled, "I don't know where you've been. I have not walked in your shoes. But I know one thing—Jesus *has* walked with you. He knows you. And He loves you right where you are. He loves you as a little sick Mormon girl."

Tears filled her eyes.

"I don't know what God has for you, Margaretta," he continued. "I know you do not grasp His grace at this moment. But I know you feel His presence, even in this illness. You know what I think?"

"What?" she sniffed.

"I think you should begin to praise God in the midst of your illness."

Praise is a concept foreign to a Mormon. Mormons sing hymns, but they do not praise. They pray, but they do not worship. The concept of simply worshiping God—speaking words of adoration and praise to Him—would find no cultural link in Margaretta. But she wanted to please God. And I think she wanted to please George.

So, pathetically, this little 79-pound Mormon girl began softly to sing the only praise words she knew:

> Praise God from whom all blessings flow,
> Praise Him, all creatures here below,
> Praise Him above, ye heavenly host,
> Praise Father, Son and Holy Ghost.

Within the Mormon community, a growing awareness of my apostasy continued to bring pressure on our marriage. I was subjected to heavy criticism. One of Margaretta's nurses told me that the stress I had caused her by leaving the Church—though I had never officially resigned, in order to spare her as much as I could—had doubtless triggered Margaretta's illness.

Meanwhile, she survived her pregnancy and presented us with a healthy daughter, Jaime. Erin by now was a precocious seven-year-old. Our home life stabilized. But I knew the time was approaching when I would be confronted by the authorities of the Church. As it happened, the confrontation came about unexpectedly.

One afternoon in October 1975 I got a call from George Eichler. He said one of his members, married to a Mormon woman, had called him. The young man's wife had invited missionaries to teach her husband about the Mormon Church. They were coming that evening and George was invited. Since he was not a specialist in Mormonism, he asked me if I would accompany him to the meeting. I agreed.

When we arrived, the missionaries were already there. Their easel was set up and they were ready to begin. Introductions were made. They said they had heard about me. George and I took our seats and I began praying for wisdom. I did not relish confrontation and I certainly did not want to badger the missionaries. On the other hand, I believed that the spiritual destiny of this family was at stake.

The missionaries seemed disconcerted at having two strangers, a pastor and a former Mormon elder, in the meeting. But they moved forward with poise. Everything they said sounded reasonable. They made no mention of any doctrine offensive to a Christian. The young man seemed to listen with an open mind, nodding and responding to the prepared questions put to him by the missionaries. I was reminded of my own first lessons twelve years earlier. How sincere and naive I had been!

I listened as long as I could, then scooted to the edge of

my chair and cleared my throat. "Excuse me, gentlemen. I'm a little disappointed in the way you are proceeding."

The older of the two men, who had been leading the discussion, glanced at his partner. "Well, Mr. Spencer, what's the problem?"

"I'm afraid you're misleading this young man."

"Perhaps you ought to do us the courtesy of allowing us to present our material before you ask questions."

"I understand how you feel. But I think you need to be very honest with this man. I want to ask you a question."

"Well, what is it?"

"Why don't you tell him that you plan to become gods?"

"What!" cried the prospective convert in alarm. "What do you mean?" He looked at the missionaries.

The younger missionary flushed in irritation. "We'll come to that!"

"That's the problem," I said evenly. "I know from personal experience that you will *not* come to it until after this man is baptized into the Mormon Church."

"We have a lot of material to cover, and we cover it in a logical sequence," replied the older man.

"But you don't mention plurality of gods anywhere in the six discussions."

"Well. . . ."

"Do you?"

Silence.

"Please," I said, "I think you owe it to all of us. Tell us now, do you believe you'll become a god?"

"The Church teaches the law of Eternal Progression."

"Do you believe you'll become a god?"

The missionary stared at me for ten long seconds, then answered quietly, "Yes. I believe that in God's economy, I will have the opportunity to progress to be as He is."

"To become a god?"

"Yes. To become a god."

There was no arguing or anger in that meeting, but an uneasy silence fell over the room. The young investigator continued to stare incredulously at the missionaries until they finally put away their material and left.

Later that night I got a call from President Jones. "Jim, I need to talk to you."

"Sure," I replied. "I'll be right over."

It was an awkward situation, I reflected in the car as I drove over to the beautiful multi-million-dollar stake building where President Jones had his office. I really liked this man and I believe he liked me. He found himself in an uncomfortable position; he didn't really thrive on conflict. But the two missionaries had called him after their confrontation with Pastor Eichler and me.

In his office, President Jones eyed me steadily. He was kind but determined. Before he could speak I said, "President Jones, I want to make this easy on you. I consider myself an apostate Mormon. There is no chance I am going to change. I can see you have no course of action open but to excommunicate me."

A look of relief crossed his face. "Well, Jim," he said, "that really is how I see things."

"I want you to know," I said, "that I bear the Church no ill will. I differ doctrinally with Mormonism and have left the Church. But I must continue to speak my mind on these matters."

President Jones shuffled some papers on his desk. "I would like you to come to the excommunication proceedings."

I was not sure I wanted to do that. Nor could I think of any good reason for doing so, since there was no possibility of reconciliation. But I wanted to cooperate.

"I suppose I could," I said hesitantly. Then something occurred to me. "I'll come on one condition."

"What's that?"

"That I be allowed time to tell why I have left the Church."

"I think that's reasonable." He paused. "Would your wife come? I mean, she wouldn't have to participate."

"What possible reason could there be for that?"

"It's Church policy."

"Oh, I see. Well, I'll ask her. Is there anything else?"

"No, I don't think so. Thank you for coming."

On the evening of the excommunication, two members of the Stake High Council, one of whom was our family doctor, came to our house beforehand to give me one last opportunity to reconsider.

Then Margaretta and I drove to the meeting, which was held at the stake building. She had agreed reluctantly to come, though I hated to subject her to further pressure or humiliation. I had no idea what was going through her mind.

In the sparsely furnished High Council Chamber, my friend Bishop Addison sat by to protect my rights and serve as my personal representative during the proceedings.

President Jones addressed the gravity of the charges against me, then told the High Council that he would permit me to speak to them about my reasons for leaving the Church.

Turning to me he asked, "Jim, will this take more than a couple of minutes?"

"Yes, President," I answered. "I think it will take about an hour."

I could tell by the faces in the room that they did not want to listen to me for an hour.

President Jones cleared his throat. "Well, this *is* an important meeting. I suppose we should give you as much time as you need."

As I looked around the room at the twelve high priests, the stake president and his two counselors, the stake secretary, Bishop Addison and my wife, it suddenly dawned on me why God had ordained this meeting. Possibly never again would I have the chance to speak to so many powerful Mormons about the good things God had done for me.

That night I preached perhaps the only Bible sermon some of those men would ever hear. I spoke of the sovereignty of God. "There is no other like Him," I said. "And brethren, I lovingly say to you, you will not become gods."

I spoke of the grace of God in saving me. Of the hopelessness I had felt. And of the cleansing and redeeming blood of Jesus Christ.

I defended the Word of God. "The Bible," I said, "is our only sure guide of faith and doctrine. It is Spirit-breathed and Spirit-preserved."

And I spoke of the fire in hell which Mormon doctrine had tried and failed to extinguish.

Behind my pleading words was a breaking heart. I loved these men from the depths of my being.

I spoke for an hour, reading entire chapters of the Bible from Galatians and Ephesians.

Finally I stopped.

Silence reigned.

And in the silence, exhaustion swept through me—a sinking weariness as I looked into the hardness of their faces, born not of maliciousness but from years of relentless indoctrination. These men had been steeped since childhood in doctrines born in hell. They had been carefully taught.

My heart broke at the raging emptiness in the hearts of

people attempting to find life in the lifeless rags of religion. There was no room in me to judge these men, only room for tears of compassion.

After a moment President Jones spoke. "Well, Jim, we certainly see your sincerity. We feel, however, that you are sincerely wrong."

Then, still addressing me: "Martin Luther was asked if he would recant. I will ask you the same question. Will you recant?"

I was slow to answer, embarrassed by the comparison.

"Brothers," I said, "I would never compare myself to Martin Luther. However, the same God who redeemed Martin Luther redeemed me. That's the only comparison. Nevertheless, I will answer as Martin Luther did: I cannot."

I was then asked to leave the room, along with my wife and Bishop Addison. I cannot imagine what the Council talked about, but it took an hour for them to decide that I was indeed apostate.

While we waited, Bishop Addison said something that struck me as ironic. He told me defensively that he thought he was as good a Christian as I was. I marveled that he could be party to my excommunication, and at the same time use my level of Christian commitment as a standard by which to measure his own.

After the three of us were invited back into High Council Chamber, my final act in the Mormon Church was to walk around the room, shake the hand of each of the high priests, look each one in the eye and, from the depths of my heart, tell him that I loved him.

Outside, Margaretta was uncharacteristically pensive. "What do you think about what happened in there?" I asked her as we walked to the car.

"I have mixed emotions," she replied slowly. "Since you've become a Christian, Jim, I've got to admit you've been a better husband and father." She hesitated. "And I'm not sure why those men have the right to sit in judgment of you. I'm not sure you've even done wrong. I guess I'm kind of confused."

As we drove home in silence, the chill wind of fall swirled leaves across the road. As they danced in the headlights, I realized that nearly two years had passed since my conversion. I wondered how many winters would pass before God would melt Margaretta's heart.

16

GOD IS FAITHFUL

The Christian evangelistic team visiting in town sprinted around the parking lot of the high school, their breath visible in the crisp January air. I watched them from my front porch. This was the second time they had been in St. Anthony.

The first time was right after my salvation. That time I had worked with another converted Mormon to bring the team to town. Now, several months after my excommunication, they were back.

Things had changed since then. Along with Margaretta's restoration to health, she had softened a bit. We continued to attend the Community Church together, plus she had not attended the Mormon church for several weeks.

Everyone I knew was praying for Margaretta. They even let her sing at Christian functions, since they believed she was on her way into the Kingdom of God and wanted to help her along.

Margaretta, in turn, had come to accept my Christian

friends. The people she "hated" turned out to be a lot of fun. One of those fun people was Katy.

Katy Cranford was a woman everyone loved. She was fearless, though sometimes she spoke first and thought later. So every time she got around my wife I got nervous. Everyone else walked around on eggshells, trying to protect Margaretta's feelings. Not Katy.

One day, for example, she whirled into the house and gasped, "It just makes me sick."

Margaretta's eyes widened. "What makes you sick?"

"Oh, I don't know," Katy said. "I always get sick when I go by a Mormon church. I mean, you can just *feel* the blackness!"

"You *can?*" Margaretta asked incredulously.

"Oh, absolutely. I mean, it's like driving by a funeral parlor!"

"Well, Katy," I interrupted. "That's really interesting. Say, by the way, how is Dale doing?"

"Don't interrupt," Margaretta said. "What do you mean you can 'feel' the blackness?"

And so it would go. It was the most unlikely friendship you could imagine. Katy was the last person I would have thought God could use to relate to Margaretta. But Margaretta just loved Katy, who could say anything to her. And usually did! They struck up a close friendship. They both loved to sing and made a strange couple doing special music at Christian functions—Katy, the effervescent autoharpist, and Margaretta, the Mormon soprano.

It was not until later that Margaretta confided to me what she was thinking during this time. She had come, after two years, to have serious doubts about the Mormon Church. Though she didn't want me to know, she had begun reading Christian tracts and literature I left lying around, careful to replace them so they appeared undisturbed. She had even looked at some of my private study materials prepared by former Mormons and cult investigators. One day, reading Dr. Walter Martin's *Kingdom of the Cults*, she got so mad she threw it across the room. But she retrieved it and read some more.

A month or so after my excommunication, Margaretta and her mother sang in the Yellowstone Stake Conference Relief Society Choir. As she described it later, she looked out that night at 2,000 dedicated Mormon faces listening to the droning of boring statistical reports, and could actually see the emptiness. Wasn't faith more than religion and church meetings? Where was the life? The joy? Did they never talk about Jesus in these meetings?

One night not long after, she and Katy sang at the Christian Center in Idaho Falls. By this time, Margaretta was beginning to search with genuine openness, recognizing that Christianity and Mormonism could not both be right.

In particular, she was interested in the concept of salvation by grace. Christians kept telling her she could not make herself acceptable to God by her good works. That if she went to heaven it would be on the merits of Christ alone. That she needed to be saved by grace. It was a concept she could not understand.

And the Christian Center meeting was strange to her. The people were joyful, all right, but they seemed too exuberant, not "reverent" enough. One little white-haired lady in particular appeared too demonstrative in her praise.

Lord, she prayed, *show me something that will prove to me what is right and what is wrong.*

After the meeting, she and Katy went out to find that the car would not start. At their sides, offering a ride and assistance, were the little white-haired lady and her husband, Alice and Bob Johnson. Later, at the Johnsons' home, Margaretta saw a poster taped to the back of a door:

> For by grace are ye saved through faith; and that not of yourselves: it is the gift of God: Not of works, lest any man should boast.
>
> (Ephesians 2:8-9)

She was shocked! What was going on here? She read it and reread it.

This can't be true, she said to herself. *And this couldn't be the King James Version. But if it were, it would be a message from God. Could He be answering my prayer?*

She could not bring herself to ask Bob or Alice Johnson about the poster. But when she got home she went into the bedroom and pulled out the worn, marked-up King James Version that she had used since childhood. She opened it nervously to Ephesians. Then she began to weep. The words were exactly the same as on the poster. God was actually speaking to her. He really did love her!

One day I came home and found her reading the Book of Mormon. Beside her book was a tract pointing out the errors in Mormonism. She didn't say anything to me, but as I looked at her, I could see hurt and confusion in her eyes. I had mixed emotions. Part of me rejoiced as I saw her begin to become aware of the truth; part of me empathized with the pain that truth brought.

Margaretta's diary from January 7, 1976, reads:

> I have come to the conclusion that the LDS Church is not true. I don't know whether to be mad or glad; I finally figured it out with the help of the Lord. I am confused as to what to do now, though.

She was ready to listen. She began to talk freely with Mike Shaw. Two Sundays in a row, as she sat in the choir at the Community Church, she listened to Pastor Shaw preach on hell. She realized she was a sinner. She knew that if she died she would go to hell. She began to open her heart to God.

And now, on January 19, 1976, the evangelistic team had returned to St. Anthony for a second engagement in the high school auditorium. This time the crowd was not as large. The main evangelist preached a hard sermon that evening. He talked about stubborn hearts that resisted the grace of God.

I was a counselor. At the end of the sermon, at the appointed moment, I stood up and walked forward with those who wanted to receive Jesus as personal Savior.

As we stood around the foot of the stage, I closed my eyes and prayed. Within moments I felt a nudge at my side. Margaretta was standing beside me with head bowed, tears streaming down her cheeks. Beside her was eight-year-old Erin, also weeping, also accepting the simple message of the gospel. That night, after two years of waiting, God gave me back my wife and my daughter.

As I looked at them, my own eyes shining with tears, I remembered that God had said, *No deals, Jim. No fleet rates. Your family is My business.* I also remembered that when I had given in to Jesus on the Sugar City Curve two years earlier, He had said to me, *Son, I love you more than you can possibly understand.* I had come to realize that in losing my life for Christ's sake, I had found it. God's timing and faithfulness were better than any plan I could have worked out.

The work Jesus had done in our hearts was well done. Every sophisticated argument was swept aside. No doctrinal snare, no demonic power, no worldly pressure could withstand the love of God. I could only marvel at God's amazing grace.

Margaretta and I looked at each other through tears. We looked at our little blonde angel staring seriously at the preacher on the stage.

Margaretta reached over and took my hand. "I've come home, Jim," she said.

EPILOGUE

Ten years have passed since the Sugar City Curve. A lot has happened in the interim. Most important, I have been called into pastoral ministry, out of which I continue to try to reach the Mormon people.

The heartland of what I call Mormondom is Utah, eastern Idaho and parts of Wyoming, Nevada and Arizona. Within these boundaries reside about three million Mormons. The area is a spiritual desert, the least Christianized section of America.

It is also, if we can believe the social statistics, one of the most hurting places in America. Yet in spite of the evident problems in Mormondom, most people have a hard time understanding why Mormonism is considered by nearly every Bible-based denomination to be a cult. It seems difficult to censure an organization that preaches qualities like family closeness, morality and patriotism. How can a religion that strives to develop the Christian characteristics of patience, decency and self-sacrifice be bad?

The answer is that only a relationship with Jesus Christ produces Christian character, and religion is a poor substitute for relationship. No social system, regardless of how orderly a citizenry it produces, is ultimately good that does not restore people to fellowship with, and bold access to, God. Our Mormon friends have been deceived into accepting a system of religion in place of redemption.

The final goal of Christianity, on the other hand, is not simply to produce people of Christian character, but to bring people into actual and vital personal relationship with God Himself. This is why Mormonism does not bear real Christian fruit. Morality and character development are no substitutes for a relationship with Jesus Christ. Obedience is no substitute for integrity. Plastic religious wings are no substitute for the Rock of Ages.

Bible Christianity, which has weathered cultish assaults for two thousand years, is charged to contend for an irreducible minimum confession of faith—"the faith which was once for all delivered to the saints" (Jude 3). That faith, simply stated, is this:

God Himself took on real flesh and entered human history, died as the full price for man's sin, declared His full divinity in His resurrection, and now redeems all who come to Him in simple faith and accept His finished work.

Mormonism, on the other hand, sets itself outside the Christian Church by declaration as well as doctrine. It reduces the divinity of Christ to mere exalted humanity; it robs the atoning blood of Christ of its power to save fully from the penalty of sin; and it replaces grace with a treadmill of self-perfection.

Christians have no right, because of some insipid, fuzzy substitute for tough love, to compromise the elements of the gospel. We deplore the doctrinal positions of Mormonism and must stand firmly against error.

At the same time, it is imperative that we view Mormons themselves with love. How vital it is to separate evil from those who are in the clutches of evil! Our job is to love the people and hate the error. This may be best summed up by the adage used as the watchword of our Mormonism newsletter, *Through the Maze:* "The truth without love is too hard; love without the truth is too soft."

Since Margaretta and I left the Mormon Church, God has blessed us. The church we pastor—Shiloh Foursquare Church in Idaho Falls, Idaho—is vigorous, and we are surrounded by loving friends and associates. In addition, I am Eastern Idaho Divisional Superintendent for my denomination.

My friend Fred Johnson is in seminary. Lee and I, sadly, do not see each other. Bill from Ricks College wrote me a long letter dissolving our former friendly relationship. Dewey Wilmot is pastoring.

God has given Margaretta and me a special love and understanding for Mormons. We have led many into a relationship with Jesus Christ. We are involved in church-planting in Idaho and Utah, and feel that a necessary blend of truth and love—toughness coupled with tenderness—is the formula needed to reach our Mormon friends.

Mormondom really needs to be evangelized. Many towns have no evangelical churches at all. Ultimately, the answer for Mormonism is the local Spirit-filled congregation. We need hundreds of evangelical churches in Mormondom.

The intense need notwithstanding, I am full of faith. I see a breakup of the social, economic and religious monopoly that Mormonism has had on Utah and Idaho for the past 140 years. We are seeing Mormons convert at a rate we could not have imagined even five years ago. Churches here, long empty and poor, are being filled to expansion. The Spirit-led Church is marching down the Wasatch

Front. I believe we are about to witness one of the greatest sovereign works of God in our time.

Appendix A

MONOTHEISM

Until recently, anthropologists have theorized that religion evolved from polytheism into monotheism. That fits in with the humanistic philosophy that man evolved from lower forms of life. Since theoretically man had no inherent knowledge of God, he invented gods incidental with his observation of nature. The prehistoric savage saw lightning strike a tree, attributed it to the gods and began to worship the lightning god. As time went on, he selected and added various gods to his religious experience. But as he grew more sophisticated, he traded in his packet of gods for a more manageable monotheistic God.

The Bible, on the other hand, teaches that man was originally monotheistic. From the very first day of creation, Adam knew there was but one Creator God. The Bible says that from original monotheism, man *de*volved into polytheism, which the Bible consistently views as deleterious.

Recent scientific evidence supports the idea of original monotheism. Anthropologists are reluctantly replacing the model of an evolving monotheism with the concept of

"High God." Researchers are finding that the most primitive tribes are not polytheistic at all, but exhibit a "belief in some kind of . . . transcendent being in whom the nature of divinity . . . is unified" (Encyclopedia *Britannica*, 1981, Vol. V, pp. 35-36; Vol. 14, p. 1042).

Appendix B

CONFUSION AMONG THE PROPHETS

Attempting to keep up with changing and contradictory Mormon doctrine is a challenge. Mormonism demonstrates that a faith built on something less than an immutable God will necessarily exhibit changing doctrine to match changing practice. Nothing in Mormonism is changeless. Major doctrines rise and fall as needed. A few interesting contradictions follow.

Polygamy. Mormonism taught polygamy until Utah was threatened with losing admittance to the Union. Then they got a "revelation" banning plural marriage. It is interesting that all the years they were polygamous, the Book of Mormon taught (in Jacob 2:24) that polygamy was abominable to God. Emma Smith, Joseph's wife, was told by "revelation" that if she did not submit to the polygamy teaching she would be "destroyed" (*Doctrine and Covenants*, Section 132). Apostle Orson Hyde claimed that Jesus married both Mary and Martha (*Journal of Discourses*, Vol. 4, pp. 259-260; *Journal of Discourses*, Vol. 2, p. 210).

Eternal Progression. Joseph Smith taught that God "is an exalted Man" (*Journal of Discourses*, Vol. 6, p. 3), and President Wilford Woodruff agreed: "God himself is progressing in knowledge, power and dominion, and will do so worlds without end" (*Journal of Discourses*, Vol. 6, p. 120). Mormon President Joseph Fielding Smith disagreed. "It seems strange to me," he wrote, "that members of the church will hold to the doctrine, 'God increases in knowledge.' . . . I think this kind of doctrine is very dangerous" (*Doctrines of Salvation*, Vol. 1, pp. 7-8).

Creation. Brigham Young said, "Adam was made from the dust of an earth, but not the dust of this earth." Joseph Fielding Smith disagreed: "The Book of Mormon, the Bible, the *Doctrine and Covenants* and *The Pearl of Great Price* all declare that Adam's body was created from the dust of the ground—that is, from the dust of this ground, this earth."

Adam-God. Brigham Young taught that Adam was the only god with whom we had to do. He defended that position by citing "how much unbelief exists in the minds of Latter-day Saints in regard to one particular doctrine which I revealed to them, and which God revealed to me—namely, that Adam is our father and God . . ." (*Deseret News*, June 18, 1873). But the October 9, 1976, issue of the Mormon-owned *Deseret News* reported President Spencer W. Kimball as saying, "We denounce that [Adam-God] theory and hope that everyone will be cautioned against this and other kinds of false doctrine."

Mormon author W. Cleon Skousen in *The First Two Thousand Years* (pp. 355-56) wrote that God is God because He has the support of other intelligent beings in the universe, and that if those beings should ever withdraw their support from Him, "he would 'cease' to be God."

Appendix C

THE BOOK OF MORMON

The most incredible example of Mormon ability to overlook error, in my opinion, is the tremendous number of changes that have been made in the Book of Mormon.

The Book of Mormon was ostensibly translated from gold plates Joseph Smith found through the direction of the angel Moroni. The Book of Mormon has been heralded as the most perfect book ever written. Mormon leadership continually affirms that it has never at any time been changed. President Joseph Fielding Smith said that only "sons of Belial" would assert that there have been thousands of changes in the Book of Mormon (*The Improvement Era*, December 1961, pp. 294-295).

The fact is, there *have* been thousands of changes in the Book of Mormon. Many are important doctrinal changes. *Anyone who wants to prove to himself that the Book of Mormon has been extensively altered can easily do so.* All he has to do is examine the 1830 edition of the Book of Mormon and compare it to the latest edition.

The 1830 edition is easily available. Brigham Young University and the University of Utah have copies. Copies are on display at major temple visitors' centers. I saw a copy displayed at the 1982 Eastern Idaho State Fair.

One of the easiest ways to see the 1830 edition of the Book of Mormon is to purchase *Joseph Smith Begins His Work*, Vol. 1, published by Wilford C. Wood (who is a Mormon) in 1958. This book is available in most Deseret bookstores. Another source is the photo-reproduced 1830 version, published by Jerald and Sandra Tanner, founders of the Modern Microfilm Company of Salt Lake City. In a work entitled *3,193 Changes in the Book of Mormon*, the Tanners reproduced the 1830 version, marked to show the changes made in the 1964 edition.

Plagiarized from the Bible. The Book of Mormon borrows copiously from the Bible. More than eighteen chapters of Isaiah are contained in it. And hundreds of parallels exist between the Book of Mormon and the New Testament—so much so that Mark Twain quipped that the Book of Mormon "seems to be merely a prosy detail of imaginary history, with the Old Testament for a model; followed by a tedious plagiarism of the New Testament" (*Roughing It*, p. 110).

The most telling proof of plagiarism is the fact that the author of the Book of Mormon copied the King James Version verbatim right down to the style of print. When the translators of the KJV translated from Hebrew to English in the Old Testament, and from Greek to English in the New Testament, they added clarifying words, italicizing them to let the reader know they were not in the original text.

The author of the Book of Mormon apparently did not realize this. Consequently, in the hundreds of verbatim passages from the Bible, the Book of Mormon italicizes the same words. Though the book was ostensibly translated from plates written in reformed Egyptian, which were copies from the original Hebrew writings, the only way to account for the italicized words is that the book was not translated from gold plates at all, but rather from a King James Bible.

Appendix D

PSYCHOLOGICAL "SNAPPING" IN THE CULTS

Certain interesting phenomena occur in the "snapped" person. For one thing, investigators find that a person's intellectual maturity seems to freeze at the point he entered the cult. Former cult members leave the cult at about the same psychological age they entered ("Information Disease: Have Cults Created a New Mental Illness?", Flo Conway and Jim Siegelman, *Science Digest*, January 1982, pp. 86-92).

I had always been an excited intellectual, feeling I was growing in maturity, experience and emotional stature. During my ten years as a Mormon, however, I had the nagging feeling I was going nowhere. Now, after nearly ten years of post-Mormon experience, I am once again experiencing the exciting feeling of personal growth.

People leaving cults also tend to experience a period of "withdrawal" in which they fight confusion. For several years after I left Mormonism, I experienced a frustrating sensation that there were places in my mind I could not go. In trying to talk to people about it, I described what seemed to be a steel band wrapped tightly around my mind.

Only after considerable ministry and prayer did I experience complete deliverance from the hold of the Mormon cult. As a final act of rejecting Mormonism, I took all Mormon literature out of my home and burned several dozen books in the desert. Only then did I feel completely free.

Studies indicate that the average rehabilitation time for former cult members is sixteen months. Long-term effects include recurring nightmares and becoming "unable to think."

RESOURCE GROUPS

Dr. Walter Martin
The Christian Research Institute
P.O. Box 500
San Juan Capistrano, CA 92675

Ed Decker
Saints Alive
P.O. Box 1076
Issaquah, WA 98027

Jerald and Sandra Tanner
Utah Lighthouse Ministry
P.O. Box 1884
Salt Lake City, UT 84110

Spiritual Counterfeits Project
P.O. Box 4309
Berkeley, CA 94704

To contact James R. Spencer or to receive the newsletter, *Through the Maze:*

James R. Spencer
Through the Maze
P.O. Box 3804
Idaho Falls, ID 83403

DOCUMENTS

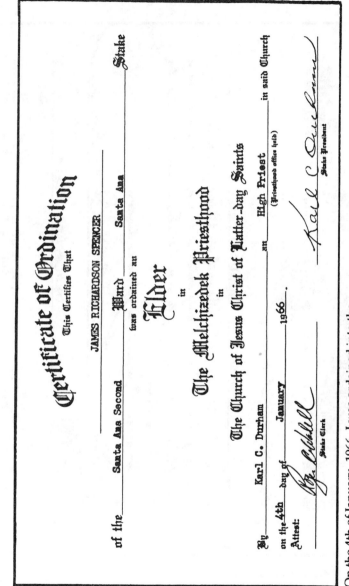

Certificate of Ordination

This Certifies That

JAMES RICHARDSON SPENCER

of the ___Santa Ana Second___ ___Ward___ ___Santa Ana___ ___Stake___

was ordained an

Elder

in

The Melchizedek Priesthood

in

The Church of Jesus Christ of Latter-day Saints

By ___Karl C. Durham___ an ___High Priest___ in said Church

(Priesthood office held)

on the ___4th___ day of ___January___ ___1966___.

Attest: _[signature]_

State Clerk

[signature] Karl C. Durham

State President

On the 4th of January, 1966, I was ordained into the
Melchizedek Priesthood, to the office of Elder.

The Church of Jesus Christ of Latter-day Saints

THE GLORY OF GOD IS INTELLIGENCE

This certifies that the bearer,

Elder   James R. Spencer

who is in full faith and fellowship with the Church of Jesus Christ of
Latter-day Saints, has been duly called and set apart as a missionary
of said Church, with authority to preach the Gospel and to administer
the ordinances thereof.

We invite all people to give heed to his message.

Karl C. Dunker
PRESIDENT

Santa Ana Stake
STAKE

2-27-66
DATE

COUNTERSIGNED BY MISSIONARY

108 FF

All missionaries who are duly called and set apart are issued a
Missionary License

TEMPLE RECOMMEND

Issued to _James Richardson Spencer_
(Please print full name)

Ward or Branch _Santa Ana II_   Stake or Mission _Santa Ana_

Female ☐   Male ☒   Priesthood _Elder_

Single ☒   Married ☐   Widow ☐   Widower ☐   Divorced ☐

The bishop or branch president will initial in his handwriting the ordinances authorized

All ordinances for the dead; also witnessing marriages or sealings	Licensed marriage _____
	Sealing after civil marriage _____
Own endowment _____	
Baptism for the dead by those over 21 years of age	Sealing to parents _____

Signatures: _James Richardson Spencer_
Applicant

George D. Church
Bishop or branch president

_____
Stake or mission president

Dated: _15 May 1966_   Note: This recommend expires April 30 next

---

If this recommend is issued for own endowment, licensed marriage, sealing after civil marriage, or sealing to parents, this section must be filled in completely

Issued to _____
(Please print full name)

Ward or Branch _____   Stake or mission _____

Female ☐   Male ☐   Priesthood _____

Single ☐   Married ☐   Widow ☐   Widower ☐   Divorced ☐

Date of birth _____

Place of birth _____   City _____   County, _____   State or Country _____

Date of baptism _____

If previously endowed give date. _____ Temple

Father's full name _____

Mother's full maiden name _____

Full name of husband or wife, or groom or bride to be _____

Date of civil marriage _____

Place of civil marriage _____

(For temple use only)

Licensed marriage ☐   Own endowment ☐   Civil marriage ☐

To be sealed only ☐

Everyone who goes through the temple must obtain a special certificate of worthiness called a Temple Recommend.